Intelligence

Daniel Cohen

Intelligence
What is it?

Designed and illustrated by Joe Hollis

M. EVANS AND COMPANY, INC.
NEW YORK, N.Y. 10017

M. Evans and Company
titles are distributed
in the United States by
the J.B. Lippincott Company,
East Washington Square,
Philadelphia, Pa. 19105,
and in Canada by McClelland
and Stewart Ltd.,
25 Hollinger Road,
Toronto 374, Ontario.

— to Harriet

Contents

1

Worm Runners and Rat Runners

For a brief but exhilarating period in the late 1950s and early 1960s it looked as if many of the vexing problems of learning, memory and all those other factors that go to make up what we call "intelligence," might soon be solved.

There was open talk about the possibility of a "smart pill" that would increase an individual's learning capacity. This heady speculation grew out of experiments with the humblest creature ever to be given a psychological test—the planarian. The planarian is a small, freshwater flatworm, usually less than a quarter of an inch long. Shaped like a fat arrow with a pointed tail, the planarian has a triangular head with two eye spots, which gives it a peculiar, cross-eyed appearance. Planarians are easily kept in the laboratory, where they live in shallow dishes of water.

In the mid-1950s Professor James McConnell and some of his colleagues in the Psychology Department of the University of Michigan began to train these simple creatures. Most psychologists at that time were of the opinion that planarians couldn't be *trained* to do anything at all, because they simply didn't have enough brain to remember anything. According to this orthodox view, all the planarians' reactions would be inborn or instinctive—flatworms just couldn't learn, they said.

One thing a planarian does do by instinct is to contract into a little ball when given a mild electric shock. Using a standard testing procedure for higher animals, Professor McConnell combined the shock with a flash of light. While planarians can detect light, a flash of light normally produces little or no reaction in them. But Professor McConnell found that after about one hundred and fifty trials, the planarian finally seemed to "get the idea" that the light and the shock were connected. After this training, the planarian would contract on the light even if there was no accompanying shock. It appeared as if the planarian had "learned" something—not much, but something.

This finding placed learning ability farther down on the evolutionary scale than most scientists previously had believed. It was an interesting though minor discovery. The next discovery in the Michigan experimental series was even more interesting, and its implications were downright revolutionary.

The structure of the planarian is simple. It can reproduce by fission, that is, by splitting in half just as the amoeba and other single-celled animals do. The planarian can also reproduce sexually, but rarely does in the laboratory. When a planarian splits, the head half of the animal grows a new tail, and the tail half grows a new head. The planarian's ability to regenerate missing parts can be stimulated artificially by cutting the creature into halves, thirds, and even smaller pieces. Each piece will grow into a full-fledged planarian within a few weeks. The limit seems to be about six pieces; after that all you have is chopped flatworm.

If the planarian's head is split in two it will grow into a two-headed planarian. If the two-headed flatworm is split in turn, the result will be a four-headed planarian, and so on. A laboratory technician with a steady hand and a keen scalpel can produce a tiny eight- or ten-headed monster. Still another trick that can be performed with planarians is to take a section of the head of one planarian and graft it onto the middle of another—this will produce a planarian with a head growing out of its side as well as a head in the normal place.

The planarian is not the only creature that can regenerate a major portion of its body, but its powers of regeneration are impressive and they have been studied very thoroughly.

However, it wasn't the planarian's well-known powers of regeneration per se that most interested Professor McConnell. He was intrigued by the possibilities such a creature seemed to offer in a study of the process of learning.

Professor McConnell cut some of his trained flatworms in half. After allowing two weeks for regeneration and another two weeks for complete recovery, he retrained the two worms that had regrown from each trained worm. The scientist found that the worms grown from heads learned to react to the flashing light after about forty trials, or a reduction of about 70 percent in normal training time. This seemed to show that the planarian had retained a considerable portion of its learning. Since the small bundle of nerve cells that can be called a planarian's brain is located in its head, the result was not too surprising. What was surprising, however, was that the planarian that grew from the tail end also learned to react to a flashing light after about forty trials. Such a result implied, and implied strongly, that memory in planarians was not something that was concentrated in the creature's brain alone, but was diffused throughout its entire body.

The next step was to cut up the regenerated worms

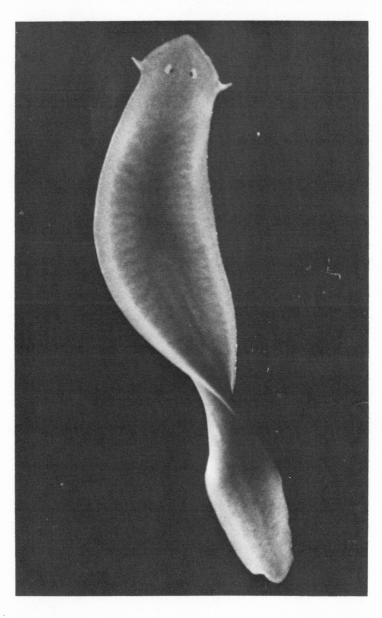

Photo of a planarian, greatly enlarged.

12   *Intelligence—What is it?*

once again. Now four worms had been made from one, and two of these new worms did not contain any part of the body of the original trained worm. Yet these new worms also learned to react to the light in less time than ordinary untrained planarians.

A real shocker came from the next experiment in this series. Planarians are cannibals and one will eat another if its victim is ground up into small enough pieces. Professor McConnell took some of his trained flatworms and chopped them up. According to the scientist, the untrained worms that were fed bits of trained worms learned to contract at a flashing light more quickly than those fed ordinary fare.

The reported results of the Michigan planarian experiments were in direct conflict with some of the basic principles of psychology and biology. The cut planarians appeared to mock the accepted view that memory was stored in the brain. At least in these very simple animals it seemed that memory was stored throughout the cells of the body.

One of the best-established hypotheses of genetics and evolution is that acquired characteristics cannot be inherited. Yet it seemed that the learning of the planarians could be passed on to descendants, though these descendants were the result of fission rather than of sexual reproduction. The idea that memory might somehow or other be inherited revived once popular theories of "racial memory"—that some of the thoughts and learning of our ancestors are part of our own biological heritage.

Followed to their logical conclusions, the Michigan planarian experiments indicated that practically everything we had previously accepted about biology and psychology was completely wrong. Professor McConnell wasn't at all upset at the prospect of overturning the entire branch of science in which he had been trained. In fact, he had a rather irreverent attitude toward science in general. He started his own scientific journal and called it *The Worm Runner's Digest*. (In psychological jargon a "runner" is an experimenter who "runs" animals through a maze—a classic animal behavior and learning test. Since this sort of experiment is usually performed with laboratory rats, experimental psychologists have often been referred to as rat runners.)

Professor McConnell sprinkled the pages of his publication with cartoons and humorous articles, which made his journal very different from the usually humorless and gray scientific journals. The professor's outspoken irreverence made him popular with a lot of people outside the scientific community and *The Worm Runner's Digest* picked up a circulation much larger than one might expect for a specialized scientific publication.

Irreverent or not, it appeared as though the planarian experiments might be getting us right to the molecular basis of memory and learning. About the time when these experiments were receiving the most publicity, three scientists were awarded a Nobel prize for figuring out the structure of the DNA (deoxyribonucleic acid) molecule. These long spiral molecules carried a genetic "message." The arrangement of compounds along the strands of the molecule determined the structure of the cell. It was through DNA that each cell "knew" what sort of cell it was supposed to be. It might be said that the DNA molecule carried the genetic "memory."

A closely related molecular chain called RNA (ribonucleic acid) was also found to play a part in the hereditary process. Professor McConnell suspected that this molecule might contain acquired sensory memories as well. He felt that in a trained planarian the memory of the flashing light followed by the shock might somehow be impressed upon the RNA of the creature's cells.

Five hundred trained planarians were killed, and the RNA extracted from their remains was injected into untrained worms. The treated worms were found to learn at a significantly faster rate than untreated worms. There was no proof that RNA actually contained the memories, just that injections of RNA appeared to improve learning capacity. Might not a substance containing RNA be used as a "smart pill" that would automatically and infallibly increase learning capacity? And if it worked for the nearly brainless planarian, why shouldn't it also work for human beings?

And then, just as it seemed that the humble planarian had opened entirely new vistas in the study of behavior and intelligence, the worms stubbornly failed to come through. A basic principle of all scientific research is that an experiment must be repeatable. Repeatability means that any group of researchers should get the same results on an experiment if they conducted it in the same way. Repeatability is necessary for several reasons. First and obviously, it helps to ensure that experimenters aren't cheating and reporting false results—cheating has been more common in science than nonscientists believe. Second, and more importantly, experiments must be repeated to make sure that the original experimenter didn't do something irrelevant to the experiment that altered the results. Yet another reason for repeating experiments is to have several different groups of researchers with different outlooks interpret the same results. Too often scientific data is like a mirror: each researcher looks at the information and sees only the reflection of his own theories. This was what happened with the planarians.

When other scientists tried to repeat the Michigan experiments they had no success at all. Not only were they unable to show that memories could be transferred from one generation of planarians to the next, most were unable to train the worms in the first place. It was particularly damaging to the planarians' reputation when Dr. Melvin Calvin, Nobel prize-winning chemist, tried to train them, failed, and decided that they really couldn't learn anything anyway. Since Professor McConnell's findings were so far out of line with previously held beliefs, most scientists simply assumed that the Michigan experiments had been badly constructed, and that the favorable results were due to a combination of misinterpretation and wishful thinking.

Professor McConnell himself became quite bitter about the attitude his scientific colleagues adopted toward his work, asking, "How do you fight someone with a Nobel prize? When there are biases anyhow, doesn't authority always win?" Professor McConnell believes that many of those scientists who tried to train planarians and failed simply did not know how to treat the worms properly. Consequently, the failure of their experiments was due to poor technique rather than faulty theory. Other experiments, he claims, show that the worms really did learn, but the experimenters failed to interpret their own data properly. Basically, Professor McConnell feels that the majority of scientists are just unwilling to accept heretical theories. His opponents naturally charge the professor with displaying exactly the same type of blindness.

The controversy started by the cross-eyed little flatworms continues to this day. Other scientists have begun tests of memory transfer with higher animals such as rats. Some of these experimenters claim a measure of success. While the subject is still highly controversial, it has, at least, become a respectable area of research.

On the other hand, the belief that the planarians might provide a new, and presumably quick method of solving some of the puzzles of memory, learning, and intelligence has evaporated. The solutions to these problems remain as elusive as they always have been, making it even more important that we understand what we know, and do not know, about the subject of intelligence.

The real base of intelligence almost certainly lies

deep within the makeup of the molecules of our nerve cells. But we are a very long way from understanding how mental processes work at the molecular, or even cellular level. To explore the problem of intelligence further we must turn from the experiments of the worm runners to those of the rat runners.

2

Mazes, Boxes, and Drooling Dogs

The word *intelligence* is not a precise and scientific term when applied to either animals or people. Many who study the psychology of animals try to avoid use of the word completely and speak instead of "adaptive behavior." But for our purposes we can give the word a rough, but useful meaning: intelligent behavior in animals is behavior that can be changed to meet changing conditions.

The little planarians may have been showing the beginning of intelligent behavior if they really "learned" to contract to a flashing light rather than to an electric shock. For animals like laboratory rats intelligence is often defined in terms of the creature's ability to learn the intricacies of a maze, or how quickly it learns to press a bar or push a switch in order to get a reward or escape a punishment. These animals are supposed to adapt their behavior to fit certain standard test conditions.

One of the earliest intelligence tests for animals was conceived by the American psychologist Edward Lee Thorndike. As his experimental subjects Thorndike used domestic cats. The apparatus for the experiment was quite simple. A cat that had not been fed for several hours was put inside a cage. Outside the cage was a plate of food. The only way the hungry cat could get at the food was by pulling a string which opened the door to the cage.

String pulling is well within a cat's physical capabilities, as anyone who has ever seen a cat play with a ball of yarn can testify. But the situation was entirely new and strange to the cat, which would not normally be required to pull strings in order to get its food. So the cat in the cage had to adapt its behavior to the unique situation. Thorndike's cats behaved very much the way common sense would lead you to believe they would. First the cats would anxiously scratch all around the cage, making a large number of ineffective motions. While scratching, the cats would, apparently by accident, pull the string, the cage door would spring open, and the cats could get the food placed outside the cage.

After being put in the cage a number of times the cats would begin to associate the string with the door, and the door with the food. They would begin to use fewer and fewer random motions. Finally they would yank the string with one simple swoop of the paw almost immediately after being put in the cage. By trial and error the cats had found the solution to their problem and had adapted their behavior to fit it.

The most sophisticated and famous development of Thorndike's method is the device called the Skinner box, named after its inventor, Harvard psychologist B. F. Skinner. Skinner wanted to construct a piece of apparatus in which learning in laboratory rats could be studied in the simplest and most objective possible manner. The device Skinner developed was a glass cage in which there is a lever or bar that can be easily depressed. In the basic Skinner box the lever or bar releases a food pellet, and the learning rate is measured in the amount of time it takes an animal—a rat, for example—to discover that

In the basic Skinner box shown here, the rat pressed down a lever which then released a small pellet of food.

pressing the bar will release the food.

In order to see whether a positive stimulus—food—is more effective than a negative stimulus—a mild electric shock—the metal floor of the Skinner box can be wired to provide a shock to the rat's feet. The shock can be avoided only when the bar is pressed. There are a large number of variations in the use of the Skinner box, and it can be adapted for use with animals other than rats. (A modified Skinner box has been extensively used in testing the behavior of pigeons.) But the basic principles of the device have remained the same: the animal must perform a simple action to get a desired result.

The Skinner box is reliable and provides a standard form in which easily repeatable experiments can be performed. But is it really testing intelligence or any other significant quality of behavior?

It has been argued that laboratory studies of this type are painfully restricted, and that the speed with which an animal learns to perform a simple but unnatural act is no true measure of intelligence. Surely a cat could adapt its behavior in more complex and varied ways than just learning to pull a string, and even a rat could do a great deal more than press a bar.

Objections to the Skinner-box type of laboratory studies of animal behavior are perfectly valid. But since intelligence has no precise scientific meaning, and the root causes of intelligent behavior are as yet completely unknown to us, the best we can do is to try and describe how patterns of behavior develop and change under certain standard conditions. In attempting to do this, the behavioral scientists have tried to isolate a single action in an experimental situation. In Thorndike's experiments the single action was the cat's ability to learn to pull a string in order to open a door; in the Skinner box it is the rat's ability to learn to press a bar.

While laboratory studies may be confining, less rigorous controls often lead to a complete misinterpretation. This can be seen most dramatically in the case of a German horse named Clever Hans, which came to the attention of scientists around the year 1900. Hans's owner, an elderly schoolmaster named von Osten, claimed that his horse could do math and spell. Indeed, von Osten said, Hans was so talented he could outperform any average ten-year-old child at such tasks.

In a simple demonstration Hans would be asked to add two and two. He would answer by pawing or tapping the ground in front of him four times. If the answers were a fraction like nine-tenths the horse would tap nine times, then hesitate and tap ten more times.

Hans would spell words by tapping the ground an appropriate number of times for each letter of the alphabet. If asked to pick a particular picture out of a group of four or five, Hans would invariably choose the correct one by tapping in front of it or by touching it with his nose.

Von Osten had his horse perform before large and admiring groups and soon news of the "genius" horse reached the ears of German scientists. Naturally they were suspicious. Animal "geniuses" of this type had been seen before. Dogs or horses that could add and spell were (and still are) popular attractions at circuses and carnivals. These performing animals have been carefully trained to obey signals from their trainers. The animals have no idea how much two and two is—they don't even understand the question. When asked "how much is two and two?" they look over at their trainers who give them the signal that means four, then they tap or bark four times. It is the signal, not the question, that stimulates the response.

A well-trained animal will react to very subtle signals which often go quite unnoticed by an audience, and a performance by one of these trained animals can be very convincing. But in the case of Clever Hans, his owner denied that he was signaling his horse or that he had trained it at all. From all accounts von Osten was an honest man, who had never attempted to make any money from his horse, but only wished to display its talents. Von Osten was so proud of the animal, he openly and enthusiastically submitted to an investigation by two psychologists. This is something no faker would do.

The psychologists immediately noticed one very disturbing thing about Clever Hans. The horse could not answer any questions if he could not see his owner. Von Osten asserted his horse became nervous and uncomfortable when he was not around and this interfered with his abilities, but the psychologists remained suspicious and began to watch von Osten instead of his horse. They soon noticed that von Osten would lean forward anxiously after asking a question, and relax and straighten up again when Hans had tapped the correct number. The horse, who kept a close eye on his owner, would begin tapping when von Osten leaned forward and stop when he straightened up. It was that simple.

Von Osten, who said he had never deliberately trained his horse to respond to signals, rejected the psychologists' explanation altogether. The psychologists were inclined to believe that the old schoolmaster was telling the truth and that he really didn't know what had happened. But when he had first begun experimenting with Hans, von Osten would reward the horse with a lump of sugar for every correct answer. The horse wanted the sugar and apparently figured out how to tap out the desired number by watching the unconscious movements of his master. Hans had "taught himself" a very effective trick. Clever Hans was indeed a very clever horse, but not in the way that von Osten and many others had thought.

Since that time a large number of other animal "geniuses" have been paraded before an admiring public by credulous or dishonest owners. Students of animal behavior remain very wary of these too clever beasts and prefer the less spectacular, but more controllable, activities of the rat in the Skinner box.

Another major problem of trying to test animal intelligence is that different animals inhabit very different sensory worlds. The right kind of test must be devised for each species. Some of the early experiments in problem solving in rats were conducted by an American psychologist named Lashley. First he tried to test the rats in a mazelike device with two alleys. The end of each alley was marked with a distinctive symbol. Behind one of the symbols was the reward of a pellet of food. Lashley wanted to see how long it would take a rat to learn which symbol hid the food. But the rats never seemed able to learn even this simple task. They continued to run up either alley at random or became discouraged and would not run anywhere. A hasty conclusion would have been that rats were too "stupid" to learn the difference between the symbols.

This seemed highly improbable and Lashley was convinced that for some reason the rats were just not using their perfectly good eyes. Lashley decided that the difficulty lay in the fact that the rat, primarily a nocturnal creature, usually navigates by touch and smell, and does not rely primarily on sight as we do. This experiment was designed to test behavior that depended upon sight. Rats in a maze would be inclined to use touch rather than sight to get around.

The scientist then came up with an apparatus in which the rats could solve the problem only by using their eyes. A test rat was put on top of a platform with two doors in front of it. At first the platform was placed close to the open doors, through which the rat could walk and obtain food. The next step was to close the doors but in such a way as the rat could open them with a push. Then the platform was moved away from the doors and the rat had to jump to get through them.

At this stage Lashley reintroduced the symbols, a boldly drawn square and triangle. If the rat jumped at the right symbol, the door snapped open and the rat was rewarded with food. If it jumped at the wrong symbol, the door remained closed, the rat got a bump on the nose, and it fell into a basket below, a thoroughly disagreeable experience. Under these conditions the rats quickly learned the correct symbol and were able to jump toward it with accuracy time after time.

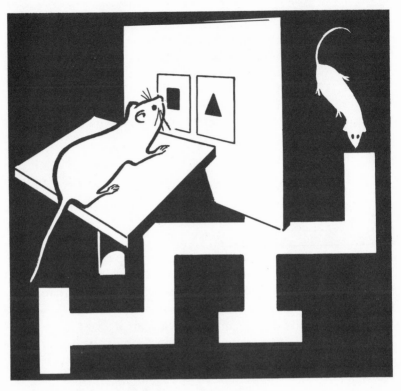

Two simplified illustrations of Lashley's devices for testing rats—the maze and jumping apparatus described on pages 24 and 25.

Animal behaviorist John Paul Scott warns: "In spite of having a variety of stimuli presented to it, an animal may respond to only one or a small part of the total situation. The fact that it does not respond to a particular stimulus under a special experimental situation does not prove that it cannot. We should neither exaggerate nor underestimate the powers which an animal has for dealing with its environment."

Thorndike's approach, and that of most American

students of animal behavior, has concentrated on testing trial and error behavior. A rather different approach to the problem of adaptive behavior was taken by the Russian physiologist Ivan Pavlov, during the 1920s and '30s. Pavlov was trying to reduce behavior to its simplest terms so that it could be more easily understood.

Pavlov had been working on the problems of digestion when he noticed that his experimental dogs, which were always fed at a particular hour, began to salivate before they were given their food, sometimes even before they could see it. Salivation, an involuntary reaction, had been adapted to the particular conditions of his laboratory. By a slow and painstaking procedure, Pavlov was able to train his experimental dogs to associate the presentation of a plate of food with a sound, usually a bell. After a while the dogs would start to salivate at the sound of the bell alone, even if no food was given. The response was completely involuntary and is what is often called a conditional or a conditioned reflex. In beginning to salivate at the sound of a bell the dogs in Pavlov's laboratory in a way had "learned" something.

Pavlov's experiment was so elegantly conceived and carefully controlled that it has been regarded as classic. Many people who know nothing about the study of animal behavior still are familiar with the term "Pavlov's dogs." Pavlov's work was and still is very influential, particularly in the Soviet Union, but also in the United States and other Western countries.

Perhaps Pavlov's work has been too influential. S. A. Barnett, in his book *Instinct and Intelligence* states: "As a result of Pavlov's work uncounted numbers of students . . . especially in medicine and psychology, have been misled into thinking that 'learning' is a simple process of establishing conditional reflexes, and that it can be fitted into an equally simple account of the nervous system. Perhaps both teachers and students found it reassuring to believe that the function of the mammalian brain, including their own, could be so simply explained. If so, they were inhabitants, no doubt temporary ones, of a fool's paradise."

Even so apparently direct and uncomplicated a reflex as salivation in a dog involves a complicated and poorly understood mass of reactions. Pavlov himself first demonstrated this complexity by presenting his dogs with a confusing set of stimuli. A dog would be trained to salivate in response to one particular musical tone, but not another. The tones were gradually brought closer and closer together on the musical scale, until they were difficult to distinguish from one another. After being subjected to this treatment a dog that had once happily submitted to the experiment would simply break down and begin running around the laboratory, cowering in a corner, or otherwise refusing to cooperate with the scientists. One might say that the dog had become "neurotic."

S. A. Barnett in *Instinct and Intelligence* writes: "The disruption of behavior, produced by certain kinds of training, reflects the complex of interacting processes which underlie the slavering of a dog awaiting a meal; probably the very ones which make a dog break down in experimental neuroses are those which, in moderation, are essential for efficient behavior."

In addition to trial and error behavior and conditional reflexes, another extensively studied form of learning in animals has been imitation. Some patterns of animal behavior are inborn while others seem to be learned by young animals mimicking the actions of adults. But it is often difficult to distinguish which actions are inborn and which are learned. Most species of birds have a characteristic song or call. When birds of some species are raised in isolation from others of their kind, they either do not sing at all or develop songs quite unlike those of their wild kin. These species of birds learn their songs by imitation. But this is not the case with all birds; for example, a chickadee raised in a laboratory without ever hearing the call of another chickadee will still utter its characteristic call.

Another interesting pattern of animal behavior is that some domestic cats catch mice while others do not. Do cats learn how to be mouse-catchers from their mothers, or is mouse-catching an inborn pattern of behavior? In broader terms, is mouse-catching the result of instinct or intelligence?

The Japanese scientist Z. Y. Kuo made a series of famous observations of domestic cats. He studied the behavior patterns of kittens that saw their mothers kill rats and mice, and kittens that did not. Of the first group almost all the kittens themselves became mouse-catchers; in the second group less than half did. Mouse-catching seems to be both inborn and learned—a product, we might say, of both a cat's heredity and environment. Like other problems of animal behavior this question does not lend itself to quick or easy answers, and manmade distinctions such as instinct, learning, and intelligence do not adequately describe the variety and complexity of nature.

We have only been able to look at a few of the high points in the study of intelligence in lower animals. As we said, many scientists hesitate to use the term at all. Is the laboratory rat in a Skinner box using the same basic processes as the mathematician working out a difficult problem? There is probably an evolutionary relationship between these two activities, but we cannot be sure.

Scientists do not really become comfortable with the concept of intelligence in animals until we go considerably up the evolutionary scale from the laboratory rat—to the level of our closest relatives in the animal kingdom, the monkeys and apes.

3

Intelligence in Apes

"If you had a penny for every time that an ape has been given an intelligence test, you would be rich indeed," wrote zoologist Desmond Morris.

No animal, save man himself, has had its intelligence probed more persistently and more thoroughly than the ape, particularly the chimpanzee. All this investigation has not been done primarily because scientists have been fascinated by ape intelligence (though the subject is a fascinating one). The reason is rather that scientists have hoped that studying the intelligence of apes can help to shed some light on the much more complicated subject of intelligence in human beings.

Why apes? The reason is obvious: they look and act more like humans than any other animals in the world. Long before Charles Darwin made us uncomfortably but undeniably aware of our close relationship to the apes, a lot of people had suspected or feared that such an association might exist. We have always had a rather ambiguous attitude toward apes. The ancient Egyptians worshiped them and held the baboon to be among the most sacred of animals. In India where they have been extremely common, monkeys still retain a semisacred status for pious Hindus. The result has been that huge numbers of monkeys have become the sort of serious nuisance that overpopulating rats and pigeons are in other parts of the world.

Historical European attitudes toward apes and monkeys were much different. Perhaps the difference came about because even in ancient times Romans and Greeks were much less likely to encounter these animals. Aristotle, natural scientist of ancient Greece, emphasized, and probably overemphasized, the physical similarities between men and apes. Pliny the Elder, a Roman natural scientist who lived at the beginning of the Christian era, commented on the "marvelous cunning" of apes, and saw them as an almost perfect imitation of man.

For Christians the apes presented some disturbing philosophical problems. All animals were supposed to have been put on earth by God in order to be of some use to man, but no one could figure out what the apes were supposed to be used for. By their appearance and actions apes seemed to be virtual caricatures of man. Since God made man in his own image, the apes were mockeries of God and man. As late as the time of Martin Luther in the sixteenth century, apes were often pictured as some kind of demon. The characterization, however, never really caught on. Snakes and even cats might be evil, but apes were just foolish.

Rather than seeing apes as demonic, the common people tended to regard them tolerantly, as symbols of human weakness and folly. In medieval Europe the term *ape* was used to denote drunkenness. One folk tradition held that apes were the descendants of a fallen branch of the human race. This tradition was not limited to Europe. In Africa some tribesmen even today believe that apes are the descendants of lazy people who ran off into the forest and began to live like animals in order to avoid work. It is said that the apes can talk but are afraid to do

so in front of people, because then the people might en-
slave them and force them to work. European Christians
arrived independently at the same sort of conclusion, that
apes were once human beings who had been degraded as
signs of divine disfavor. This was Darwin's theory turned
upside down: rather than man's having "risen" from the
apes, the apes had "fallen" from man.

Medieval legends, which often took extreme license
with the Bible, reflected these common beliefs. One story
told of how God visited Eve after her expulsion from the
Garden of Eden. He asked her how many children she
had. Eve had so many that she was afraid God would
think that she was enjoying her newly acquired knowledge of the pleasures of the flesh too much. So Eve hid
some of her children. God, of course, detected the decep-
tion and in retribution turned some of her children into
demons and others into apes. In one form or another the
idea of apes as fallen and sinful men persisted through
the centuries. Monkeys and apes were never classed
among the most noble of God's creations; which partly
explains why people in the nineteenth century found
Darwin's idea of man actually being related to the apes
so disturbing and distasteful.

Speculation about the position of apes as a debased
kind of man started well before Western man had any important encounters with the anthropoid or manlike apes
(a group that includes the chimpanzee, gorilla, orangutan,
and sometimes the gibbon). Beliefs were based on infre-
quent observations of small monkeys, baboons, and Barbary apes. A small colony of Barbary apes on the rock of
Gibraltar are the only wild primates in Europe today.
When people ran into real anthropoid apes they simply
assumed that the creatures *were* some sort of wild man. A
classic meeting between man and anthropoid ape took
place early in the sixth century B.C. The Carthaginian explorer Hanno, who was leading an expedition along the

west coast of Africa, found an island that was "full of savage people, the greater part of whom were women, whose bodies were hairy, and whom our interpreters called Gorillae. Though we pursued the men, we could not seize any of them; but all fled from us, escaping over the precipices, and defending themselves with stones. Three women were taken however; but they attacked their conductors with their teeth and hands, and could not be prevailed on to accompany us. Having killed them, we flayed them, and brought their skins with us to Carthage."

There is some dispute as to whether these "hairy women" were really gorillas or chimpanzees or perhaps some form of now extinct African ape. Since the skins, along with Carthage itself, have long since disappeared, the dispute can never be resolved. The point is that, to Hanno, these creatures looked and acted human enough to be considered human, though a distinctly savage and inferior type of human.

Through the centuries other explorers and travelers reported similar tales. Ancient and medieval natural histories recorded numerous forms of "wild men" that almost certainly derived from poorly described sightings of anthropoid apes.

It wasn't until the seventeenth century that Europeans began to get any really accurate information about the great apes. A few of these creatures were brought to Europe as pets and curiosities by explorers and soldiers. When the animals died, as they usually did very quickly, the remains sometimes found their way into the laboratories of physicians and anatomists. A London physician named Edward Tyson was the first Westerner known to have dissected an anthropoid ape. The results of his dissection, accompanied by a series of excellent anatomical drawings, were first published in 1769. The animal clearly was a chimpanzee, though Tyson called it a "pygmie." The London physician was much impressed by the

This is how Beeckman visualized an orang-utan in 1714. He called it "oran-ootan."

size of the creature's brain, which he thought was as large in proportion to the size of its body as was a man's. From his examination of the creature's larynx Tyson could see no reason why it should not talk. He concluded that his "pygmie" was a being somewhere halfway between ape and man.

Others were inclined to rate the anthropoid ape even higher. The eccentric Scottish jurist and pioneer anthropologist Lord Monboddo (1714–1799) was a pre-Darwinian evolutionist and much interested in the intelligence of anthropoid apes. He believed that the "orang-utang" (a term which might have meant any of the great apes) was more advanced than many primitive people. One of Lord Monboddo's favorite theories was that with the proper training these apes would be able to learn to talk.

But it was Charles Darwin who in the mid-nineteenth century gave the apes their greatest boost in status, and provided mankind with a rude and ego-shattering shock, from which we have never quite recovered. Darwin scrapped the entire notion of man as a product of special creation and asserted that our mental and physical difference from the apes was only a matter of degree. Darwin's most effective disciple, the brilliant and contentious Thomas Henry Huxley, twisted the knife by saying that the difference between anthropoid apes and monkeys was much greater than the difference between anthropoid apes and man.

In the angry and emotional debate which swirled about Darwin's theories, his opponents did not dare make much of a case of the physical differences between men and apes, as the physical similarities were much too obvious. They did, however, insist that there were vast and unbridgeable mental, moral, and spiritual differences between men and apes. The moral and spiritual differences were not very fruitful areas for discussion, since these

A contemporary carica-
ture of Charles Darwin.

were entirely matters of opinion. But in the matter of
mental differences, the antievolutionists thought they had
some telling points to make.

Sir Richard Owen was the leading anatomist of his
day and a determined and ferocious antievolutionist. Darwin once conceded that Owen was the only man who had
ever made him angry. Owen studied the anatomy of anthropoid apes about as thoroughly as any man in the
nineteenth century, and he concluded that there were so
many fundamental differences between the brain of a gorilla and the brain of a man that the two species could
not possibly be related. Huxley disagreed and, in a paper
published in the *Natural History Review* of 1861, won his
case in the eyes of most of his fellow scientists.

Language presented a more serious problem for
those trying to establish a close relationship between man

and the apes. The use of language had always been considered one of the accomplishments that set man apart from the animals. Darwin contended that monkeys and apes had the ability to communicate with one another by means of simple sounds. Some of his more enthusiastic followers thought they had discovered a whole ape language.

In the late 1890s Richard L. Garner studied the speech of monkeys and apes and reported that he found they possessed a vast and complex language. He wrote in his book *Gorillas and Chimpanzees:* "There are other sounds which are easily identified but difficult to describe, such as that used to signify 'cold' or 'discomfort'; another for 'drink'; another referring to 'illness'; and still another which I have good reason to believe means 'dead' or 'death' . . . the sounds uttered by these apes have all the characteristics of true speech."

In their haste to raise the status of the apes, the evolutionists had gone well beyond the known facts. At the beginning of the nineteenth century the known facts about the behavior of the great apes were very few. The anatomy of apes had been well explored, but a dissected specimen revealed nothing of how a living ape behaved.

The whole idea of studying animal behavior at all was a rather novel one, and it was an area of study fraught with moral judgment and sentimentality. If animals, and particularly apes, were close relatives of man, then either man was a brute, or the animals were more human. The early students of animal behavior opted for the human side of animals, and attributed to animals a variety of human emotions and motives which really impeded the study of animal behavior. Right now the fashionable view is that man is more of a brute, but this interpretation may be no nearer the truth than the earlier one.

Studying the behavior of anthropoid apes was particularly difficult for there were very few apes around Europe to be studied. Most scientists had to depend upon travelers' tales for their information on ape behavior, which led to a flock of wild, but widely repeated, misconceptions. The most persistent one held that the gorilla has a basically vicious temperament. Stories about huge "killer" apes were spread by hunters and explorers, and faithfully echoed by nineteenth- and early twentieth-century scientists. Even today the vision of the gorilla as some sort of King Kong type of monster lingers on in the public's imagination, though we now know that for all its size and strength the gorilla is an inoffensive creature.

Performing monkeys and apes were often put on display in carnivals and circuses. They were able to master a large number of complicated tricks, and certainly appeared "intelligent." However, other animals, dogs, horses, and even pigs and birds were also regular performers. There was no lack of "wonder dogs" and "genius horses," so that the mere fact that an animal was trainable told little about its intelligence.

Despite the tremendous interest in the possible intelligence of the apes that Darwinian theory had awakened, there was really very little scientific study of the subject until 1912. In that year the Prussian Academy of Science bought nine wild chimpanzees and sent them to a laboratory in the Canary Islands, to be studied by a young psychologist named Wolfgang Köhler. Two of the chimps died, but Köhler devised a variety of experiments to probe the mental capacities of the seven survivors. Unfortunately, the laboratory was opened shortly before the outbreak of World War I, and it was closed when the Germans were defeated in 1918. Seven more years passed before Köhler was able to publish the results of his pioneering studies.

Much of what Köhler learned seems rather commonplace and obvious to us today. But one must remember that before he started his observations no scientist had ever carried on extended experiments on chimp behavior, and people were operating with all sorts of incorrect notions about how chimps should behave.

Köhler found that if a banana was tied high out of a chimpanzee's reach and the animal was given a stick, it would use the stick to knock down the banana. Chimps would also quickly discover how to use a stick to pull in a banana that had been placed beyond their reach outside their cage. One chimp learned how to make a stick longer by jamming a smaller stick into a larger tube. The same chimp, when it wanted to fit a board inside of the tube but found the board too wide, tried to chew down the end of the board in order to make it fit. The chimp had the right idea, but he was never able to chew the board down to a proper size.

Köhler's most famous experiments involved box stacking. If food was tied high out of a chimp's reach, and the chimp was given two or more boxes, would it be able to build a platform from which it could reach the food? The chimps could do this, though Köhler was not much impressed by the way they did it. Köhler's chimps didn't seem to know whether they were building a stable tower or an unstable one. The chimps were constantly falling over trying to climb up badly balanced piles of boxes. Some chimps even tried to build their towers higher by lifting out the box on which they were standing. This, according to one scientist, was "the traditional feat of lifting oneself up by one's bootstraps."

Later observers of chimp behavior repeated these experiments and found that the chimps were much better at box stacking than Köhler had believed. One of the problems with testing chimpanzee behavior is that chimps are highly individualistic animals. A task that is impossible for one is easy for another; thus generalizing about their behavior is always uncertain.

The object of the Köhler experiments was to see if the primates displayed *insight*. This term implied planned and organized behavior, surveying the situation before acting. Insight was postulated as a higher form of behavior than the trial and error method of problem solving often seen in lower animals. Köhler found that his chimpanzees did indeed behave with insight.

Here we confront one of the classic problems in the study of behavior and intelligence—how an action is to be interpreted. Since Köhler's time the whole concept of insight has been subjected to a great deal of criticism by those who say that insight is more in the eyes of the observer than in the actions of the animal, more an interpretive reaction than a scientifically objective fact. The philosopher Bertrand Russell once remarked that animals in American psychological tests seem to learn through trial and error, while the same animals when tested by Germans sit and wait for a flash of insight.

The most important revision of the insight theory was made by Drs. Harry and Margaret Harlow of the University of Wisconsin in their investigation of monkeys. In an article "Learning to Think," which appeared in *Scientific American* in 1949, the Harlows described the procedure.

One of the first experiments was a simple discrimination test. The monkeys were confronted with a small board on which lay two objects different in color, size, and shape. If a monkey picked up the correct object, it was rewarded by finding raisins or peanuts underneath. The position of the objects was shifted on the board in an irregular manner from trial to trial, and the trials continued until the monkey learned to choose the correct object. The Harlows wrote: "The unusual feature of the experiment was that the test was repeated many times, with several hundred different pairs of objects. In other words, instead of training a monkey to solve a single problem, as had been done in most previous psychological work of this kind, we trained the animal on many problems, all of the same general type, but with varying kinds of objects."

What happened was that the monkeys first fumbled around with the objects, learning by trial and error. But as they gained experience with this sort of problem the monkeys got better at solving it. Eventually, say the Harlows, the monkeys showed "perfect insight." Once they found the right object, they rarely made an error afterward. If they picked the wrong object they shifted immediately to the correct one and then rarely made an error.

To the Harlows these actions demonstrated that "the trial-and-error and insight are but two different phases of one long continuous process. They are not different capacities, but merely represent the orderly development of a learning and thinking process."

The same problems were tried on nursery school children, aged two to five. The children did better than the monkeys, though the smartest monkeys learned faster than the dullest children. The important discovery was that the process by which monkey and child learned to solve the problems was basically the same.

The Harlows call this process the formation of a "learning set." They wrote, "The subject learns an organized set of habits that enables him to meet effectively each new problem of this particular kind." Tests also indicated that monkeys had a very good memory for the learning sets. Some of the monkeys were retested a year after they had first mastered the problems, and were able to recapture their old skill in a few minutes or hours of practice, though it may originally have taken them several weeks to attain the skill.

The Harlows' work and most of the other investigations of primates would probably never have taken place had it not been for Robert Mearns Yerkes of Harvard University. Before World War I, Yerkes had studied the behavior of a variety of animals, from mice to pigs, but his real passion was the behavior of apes. The difficulty was that there were very few apes available for study, and facilities for studying them virtually did not exist. Many captive apes survived for only a short time because they were in poor shape when they arrived in America, and no one knew how to take care of them properly.

Yerkes obtained two chimpanzees of his own, though it cost him every penny he had in the bank, and he studied them as best he could. His dream was to establish a laboratory where a large number of chimpanzees could be kept and bred for research purposes. But it wasn't until 1930 that Yerkes managed to turn his dream into reality, with the establishment of a primate laboratory in Orange Park, Florida. Orange Park became the model for the dozens of primate study centers that now exist in America.

Another approach to primate behavior began in the 1920s when a young South African anatomist named Solly Zuckerman started studying the social behavior of a colony of baboons in London's Regent's Park Zoo. Zuckerman had been interested in these animals in his homeland and when he returned to South Africa in the 1930s, he put his London training to good use: he conducted the first truly scientific study of the social life of monkeys and apes. Zuckerman concluded in his book *The Social Life of Monkeys and Apes*, "sociologists have found it easy to convince themselves that the behaviour of apes supports whatever view they may happen to hold about the origins of human society." Despite many advances, the same criticism can often be applied to the uses made of studies of primate behavior today.

Scientific investigation of the behavior and intelligence of man's closest relations in the animal world has not been going on for very long; but it is an area in which information has accumulated rapidly. The first fact psychologists noted about chimpanzees is that they are extremely good at learning to use tools. A variety of experimenters found that using a key to open a locked box or cupboard in which food had been hidden was mere child's play to a chimpanzee. More complicated fastenings didn't faze them either, and chimps soon learned how to open a cabinet that had been secured with a whole series of bolts and catches.

A more difficult task required the animals to put a stick into a hole, press it to tilt a board, then take the stick out, put it into a second hole, and press and tilt again. With each tilt a single grape was released and rolled down a long zigzag path to the waiting animal. The chimps found this sort of problem a bit more difficult to figure out, and it took them about three sessions before they had the procedure down pat. Says zoologist Desmond Morris of this performance: "It is still brilliant by other animal standards." Morris also points out that while such activities might seem trivial when compared to the

Desmond Morris (above) proved that chimpanzees easily learned to use tools and perform tasks for rewards. The chimpanzee on the left knows there will be a reward for opening the locked box.

complicated routines learned by performing chimpanzees, stage animals have been carefully trained and rehearsed, while the chimps being tested had to figure out the solutions to problems all on their own.

Scientists also found that chimpanzees could learn how to handle symbols, in one case: money, or its equivalent, white poker chips. Dr. John Wolfe of the Yale Laboratories of Primate Biology tested them on a device that was dubbed the chimp-o-mat—a modified slot machine. If a white poker chip was inserted into the machine a grape would drop out. That was an easy first step and the chimps quickly mastered the use of the device, grabbing eagerly for white chips when they were offered.

The next step was to introduce brass slugs into the experiment. Though the slugs were the same size and shape as the poker chips, when inserted into the chimp-o-mat, nothing happened. The animals soon learned the difference between slugs and chips and, when given a choice, they would immediately take the chips and ignore the slugs.

Dr. Wolfe then constructed a device called a work machine. When the chimps lifted a handle which was quite heavy for them, a slot would open and they could reach inside of the machine and extract one grape. Eventually the grapes were replaced by white poker chips. The chimps worked just as hard to get the chips as they had to get the grapes themselves—even though the chimp-o-mat was nowhere around, causing their food reward to be delayed. Some were better at waiting than others. A few kept on working at such a frenzied pace that keepers feared they would injure themselves.

The activity around the work machine gradually tapered off. If the chimps had a large supply of chips already on hand they would only lift the handle a few times before losing interest.

Dr. Wolfe added a further refinement to the experiment: different colored poker chips. Blue chips brought two grapes from the chimp-o-mat, red chips were worth a drink of water, and a yellow chip inserted into the slot got the chimp a piggyback ride on the shoulders of one of the psychologists.

The results were as expected. The once treasured white chips were now passed up in a rush to get blue chips. Thirsty chimps chose red chips over either white or blue, and bored but sated chimps opted for the yellow chips and a ride around the laboratory.

Chimpanzees have also been given some of the same sort of intelligence tests that are given to human children. Obviously chimps can't read directions or match lists of words, but many of the tests used on very young children involve such activities as putting square pegs into square holes. Chimpanzees are very good at tests of this type.

It has often been asserted that a chimpanzee is as intelligent as a four-year-old child, but such comparisons are really meaningless. It is hard enough to assess the intelligence of one human being compared with another, or even to agree on what intelligence is supposed to be. To try to make a comparison between two entirely different species is an exercise in futility, though it is done all too often.

Infant chimpanzees develop much faster than human infants do. A four-month-old chimpanzee can not only walk but climb. It has much better muscular control than a four-month-old human infant, who may not yet be able to turn over. Obviously the chimpanzees will be way ahead on any tasks involving manual dexterity and muscular coordination. Later on though, while the chimps are still more coordinated than two- or three-year-old children, they tend to lose interest in tests more quickly, and their comparative performance goes down. Once a human child begins to understand and use language, all hope of comparison goes out the window.

The problem returns to language, a question that concerned so many early students of animal behavior. If language is a sign of intelligence, why doesn't the chimpanzee, generally considered the most intelligent of animals, have a language—or does it? There is still a great deal of dispute among anatomists as to whether the chimpanzee possesses the physical equipment to make a more complex range of sounds than it does. Some scientists have tried to bypass this problem and teach a chimpanzee or some other anthropoid ape human speech.

Probably the most sustained and well-known attempt to teach a chimp to speak was made by Keith and Cathy Hayes, both of whom worked at the Yerkes Laboratory of Primate Biology. They raised a chimpanzee in their home from infancy, and lavished it with even more attention than is given to the average human infant. Stories about the Hayeses and their experiences with their chimpanzee, Vicki, are so well known that there is no need to repeat them here in any detail. Basically what they found was that Vicki mastered mechanical skills easily, but did not even come close to understanding language. In order to teach Vicki to say words like "mama" for Cathy, "papa" for Keith, and "cup," a signal that she wanted a drink, the Hayeses actually had to manipulate the animal's lips at first. Even after she had mastered the words, Vicki's "pronunciation," if it can be called that, was very poor. The experiments ended abruptly when Vicki died at the age of six and a half. At that time she was learning only her fourth word: "up."

In their attempts to find more effective ways of teaching and controlling Vicki, the Hayeses took the ape to schools for the mentally retarded. At one institution Vicki was tested on the social maturity scale. This examination covered self-care, locomotion, play, and communication, and was not strictly speaking an intelligence test. In total, the ape scored eight months ahead of the normal human child of her age (Vicki was three at the time). But the total score was very misleading. The ape scored very high on any part of the test requiring manual skill, but her language development was equal only to that of a one-year-old.

"When all this was added up," says writer Emily Hahn in her book *On the Side of the Apes*, "the answer seemed to be that what the Hayeses had was a chimpanzee, not a child."

As far as teaching an ape human language, the Hayeses' experiment, and a few others that have been conducted along similar lines, have to be regarded as qualified successes at best. Does this mean that language, which seems to be such a vital part of what we call intelligence, is beyond the abilities of the most intelligent of lower animals? Perhaps not, for these past attempts to teach apes to speak may just have been going at the problem the wrong way. Perhaps speech, that is, vocalization is not the best way for apes to communicate.

Robert Yerkes had suspected this and, in his book *Almost Human*, he speculated: "Perhaps they [the apes] can be taught to use their fingers, somewhat as does the deaf and dumb person, and thus helped to acquire a simple, nonvocal 'sign language.'" This suggestion was very reasonable in view of the apes' well-known skill in imitating human gestures, but surprisingly it wasn't until the late 1960s that there was any concentrated attempt to follow it up.

In June 1966 a husband-and-wife team of psychologists, Allen and Beatrice Gardner of the University of Nevada obtained a young female chimpanzee they named Washoe. The Gardners began a rigorous program to teach Washoe to communicate by means of the American Sign Language, or ASL, the standard deaf and dumb language used in this country.

Washoe lives in a trailer in the Gardners' yard, and

she spends almost all of her waking hours in the presence of one or more human companions. The humans not only communicate with Washoe by sign language, they also communicate with one another that way while in the presence of the chimpanzee. The reason is to convince Washoe that sign language is the only way to communicate.

The experiment has quite naturally attracted a great deal of attention, and in order to keep Washoe from being constantly distracted by reporters and other curious visitors, the Gardners have kept their protégé under tight security. Films of the young ape show her standing in front of a refrigerator signing "open food drink," and indicating that she wants something quickly by signing "please come give me hurry more."

Washoe has learned over forty signs and is still learning. The Gardners do not claim that she has absolutely mastered every one of the signs she uses. For example, she signs "more" by striking her fists together over her head. The proper ASL sign is made by striking the fists together in front of the chest. The excitable chimp often uses the wrong signs, or fails to use signs at all. But on balance, the Gardners feel that they have achieved a limited but definite method of communicating with a nonhuman species.

How far Washoe can go in learning sign language is at present unknown and, of course, this is only the first attempt. Later investigators may evolve more efficient methods of teaching chimpanzees sign language.

Another approach to nonvocal communication with a chimpanzee has been tried by David Premack of the University of California. Premack's subject is an adult chimpanzee named Sarah. Rather than communicating with speech or sign language Sarah is learning to "write," not in letters but in symbols.

For the experiment Premack uses a magnetic board

and a number of plastic symbols mounted on metal bases. It was easy for the chimpanzee to learn that a square stood for "banana," and a triangle for "apple." It was harder for her to learn how to use the symbols for such words as "on" and "give," but after a while she was able to construct short "sentences," by attaching the symbols to the magnetized board in a particular order. When the chimp's trainer, Mary Morgan, gave her an apple, Sarah could describe the event by writing the following "sentence" on her magnetized board: "Mary give apple Sarah."

These experiments with man-chimpanzee communication are both ingenious and interesting, but how significant are they? Most psychologists believe that there is a definite relationship between language and intelligence, and that there can be no high order of intelligence without language. Do the experiments properly display chimpanzee intelligence, and will it be possible to increase the intelligence of apes if we can teach them a human language? The whole area of language and intelligence is so filled with controversy and uncertainty that we are not able to answer such questions at present. Some scientists even think that experiments like the one with Washoe are merely superior forms of animal training and that Washoe signing "please come give me hurry more" tells us nothing more about chimpanzee intelligence than the elaborate antics of performing apes.

Rather than attempting to judge chimpanzee intelligence by human standards, that is, by seeing how much we can get them to act as we do, we might be better off judging them by their own standards. How well do chimpanzees use the intelligence they possess in coping with the problems of their own environment?

Scientists felt for a long time that it was useless to hope to study the behavior of chimpanzees or any of the other anthropoid apes in the wild. Apes lived in inaccessible forests and jungles, were elusive and, worst of all, they and the other beasts that roamed the forests and jungles were thought to be extremely dangerous. At the end of the nineteenth century Richard L. Garner tried to study chimpanzees in the wild. He prepared for his study by constructing a massive cage in the jungle, then locking himself inside armed with a rifle, revolver, and heavy knife. Thus safe from "the fierce and stealthy beasts of the jungle," Garner settled down to make his observations. Not surprisingly, he found that very few chimps ever came near enough to his cage for him to do much observing. He did listen to the sounds they made, though, which helped him evolve his incorrect theories of chimpanzee language.

Our entire view of the life of wild chimpanzees was changed by a young Englishwoman named Jane Goodall. In 1959 she began what was to turn out to be years of extended observation of wild chimps. She abandoned all of the traditional notions about "ferocious" wild apes. Alone, and armed only with enormous patience, Jane Goodall was able to win the confidence of the normally elusive apes and bring back the first reliable and close-up observations of chimpanzee life in the wild. She found that the wild apes displayed a considerable degree of what we would call "intelligent behavior." They didn't need human training or an artificially "enriched environment" to teach them.

One of her most startling discoveries came when she saw chimps stripping the leaves off twigs, and then using the bare twigs to extract termites from holes in the ground. The chimps regard termites as a great delicacy. In doing this the chimpanzees had made and used a simple tool. Prior to this discovery man had been considered the only tool-making animal. The late Dr. Louis Leakey, anthropologist, paleontologist, and Jane Goodall's first patron quipped: "I feel that scientists holding to this definition are faced with three choices: they must accept chimpanzees as man, by definition; they must redefine man, or they must redefine tools."

Another pioneer in the study of the behavior of apes in the wild is the American animal behavioralist George Schaller. Schaller took on an even more imposing challenge, the mountain gorilla, an animal with an ancient reputation for ferocity and brute strength. Schaller too was usually alone and unarmed, and though the huge primates gave him a few nervous moments, they never harmed him. Schaller has shattered, hopefully for all time, the myth of the killer ape. He found gorillas to be generally shy, nonaggressive, and basically lazy animals. But he was not too impressed with their intelligence. Gorillas seemed to be far less adaptable and curious than the chimpanzees.

Both Goodall and Schaller, and the dozens of other students of the behavior of apes in the wild who have followed their lead, have found that the apes do communicate by a variety of sounds and gestures. This communication seems to be at a fairly simple level, and whether one wishes to call it a language or not depends pretty much on how one defines the word language. Apes seem to be quite good at communicating emotions, and mother apes are able to teach their young which foods to eat and which to avoid. But so far there is no evidence that apes can communicate more complicated ideas. Certainly there is no indication that they are even remotely capable of transmitting what we call civilization or culture.

The evidence that has accumulated over the last half century from laboratory and field studies should have placed apes, particularly chimpanzees, at the very pinnacle of the animal intelligence scale, the undisputed I.Q. champions, next to man, of course. But their supremacy has been challenged from a most surprising source: the dolphins and whales.

4

The Big Brains
of the Sea

We had assumed, rather egotistically, that apes had to be the most intelligent of the animals because they are the ones that look most like us. Therefore it came as something of a surprise that over the last decade or so there has been a good deal of talk that dolphins and whales may be more intelligent than chimpanzees, and perhaps even more intelligent than man.

Superficially at least, a dolphin looks more like a herring than it does a man. The resemblance, however, is only skin deep. The members of the order Cetacea, to which the dolphins and whales belong, are mammals; they are all air-breathers, all warm-blooded, and all bear their young alive and suckle them on milk, as do all other mammals.

Somewhere well back in their evolutionary history, the ancestors of modern whales and dolphins were land-living carnivores that returned to the sea. They probably began by eating fish and shellfish found on shore, then started diving into the water after their food, and finally evolved to the point where they did not have to return to land at all, not even to bear their young.

Right now some scientists suspect that the polar

bear, which spends a great deal of time in the water and is an excellent swimmer, is just beginning the same sort of evolutionary journey. This journey may be cut short unless rich "sportsmen" can somehow be persuaded or prevented from slaughtering the rare animals for no better purpose than to have a stuffed specimen to adorn their dens. The seal has already evolved more than halfway back to the sea, a fact that is obvious to anyone who has ever watched a seal clumsily moving around on land.

Very little is known for sure about the evolutionary history of the Cetacea, but we do know that life in the sea calls for a very different set of adaptations than life on land. Feet are useless, and in dolphins and whales the front limbs have evolved into flippers, while the back ones have disappeared entirely. The Cetacea became more streamlined, lost their hair, and their nostrils, now reduced to a single blowhole, moved to the tops of their heads. Great size can be a disadvantage on land where a creature must carry around all its weight against the pull of gravity, but size is not necessarily a handicap in water, which supports weight. As a result, the largest creature that ever lived, an animal far larger than the largest dinosaur, is the blue whale which, while rare, still lives today. Even small whales like the dolphin weigh hundreds of pounds, and dwarf all but the largest of land-living animals.

The order Cetacea is divided into two living suborders, the toothed whales and the baleen, or wholebone, whales. The blue whale and most of the other really huge whales are of the baleen variety. Their mouths are lined with plates of fibrous material called baleen, or whalebone, which strains tiny animals from the water. These largest of the world's creatures sustain themselves by eating some of the smallest.

The baleen whales are of less interest to students of animal intelligence than are the toothed whales. Among the toothed whales are the dolphins and particularly the bottle-nosed dolphin which has been studied most extensively. There is also the killer whale, a larger toothed whale which recently has been shedding its reputation for unbridled ferocity and gaining one for intelligence. Finally there is the sperm whale, largest of the toothed whales, and the only one that rivals the baleen whales in size. Most authorities on whales believe that the toothed whales are more intelligent than the baleen whales, though in truth we know so little about the behavior of baleen whales that we may be grossly underrating their intelligence as a result of our own ignorance.

There have been tales about the intelligence of dolphins for centuries. Sailors reported how dolphins drove off attacking sharks by ganging up on them and bumping them with their noses. Aristotle recorded an incident in which a group of dolphins tried to save one of their number who had become trapped. Occasionally sailors told of dolphins that would guide them through treacherous straits, and exhausted swimmers said that they had been pushed toward shore by a friendly dolphin and thus saved from drowning.

These stories indicated that the dolphins, despite their fishy shape, were highly intelligent animals. But such anecdotes don't really amount to much. There are volumes of stories about dogs or horses or camels that displayed even more "intelligent" behavior. What really stimulated the interest of scientists in the question of dolphin intelligence was the size of the creature's brain.

The dolphin has an enormous brain. The average brain of a bottle-nosed dolphin weighs about 3¾ pounds. An average human brain weighs only three pounds, and the brain of the chimpanzee weighs about half that of an adult human being.

Such comparisons are not really fair either to man or the chimpanzee. The brain of an adult elephant weighs as much as thirteen pounds, far more than that of a chimpanzee, a man, or a bottle-nosed dolphin. Elephants are thought to be somewhat intelligent but not as intelligent as such a brain size might indicate. The key is the animal's total size: an elephant can weigh up to six tons. The sperm whale has the largest brain of any creature that lives now or has ever lived. The average brain of an adult sperm whale weighs twenty pounds. But an adult male sperm whale also grows to a length of more than sixty feet, and can weigh one hundred tons. The blue whale, largest creature ever living, grows at least a third bigger than the largest sperm whale, but it has a smaller brain.

Thus, sheer brain weight is not the only factor scientists consider. A second measurement is the ratio between a creature's total body weight and the weight of its brain. Actually a number of small and rather lowly animals—the mole, the shrew, the marmoset—have more favorable body-brain weight ratios than man does. But these little creatures don't really figure in the intelligence sweepstakes, because the structures of their brains are considerably different from those of the larger-brained animals. It is fairly safe to assume that very small brains are not capable of high intelligence no matter what the body-brain weight ratio.

After eliminating this competition, man does come out on top of the chart. The ratio of man's total body weight to the weight of his brain is approximately 50 to 1, whereas with the elephant the ratio is closer to 1000 to 1. The dolphin has a highly respectable body-weight to brain-weight ratio of 90 to 1. The blue whale, on the other hand, has such an enormous body that its body-weight to brain-weight ratio is a staggering 8500 to 1.

Using the body-weight-brain-weight ratio we can construct a neat chart with man on top, the chimpanzee beneath, the dolphin a little farther down, and the great

ANIMALS RANKED ACCORDING TO

A	B	C
TOTAL BRAIN WEIGHT	RATIO OF BRAIN WEIGHT TO BODY WEIGHT	RATIO OF BRAIN WEIGHT TO STEM WEIGHT

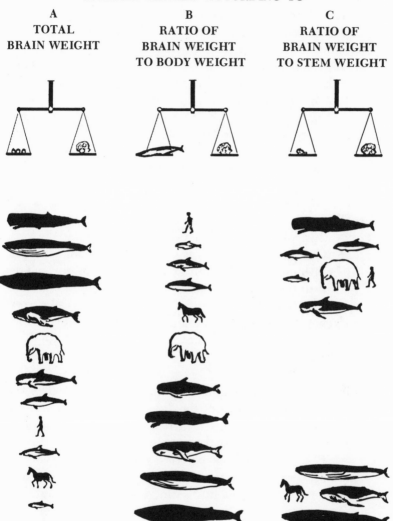

Note that the sperm whale tops Columns A and C. Man should not really be shown topping Column B—it should be the marmoset or the tiny shrew.

whales way down near the bottom. But, as we have already seen with the shrew and the mole, even the ratio does not tell the whole story. A large percentage of a whale's body is fat, and it would not seem that much brain tissue would be needed to control fatty tissue. Thus the whale's tremendous weight tends to unbalance the possible meaning of a weight-ratio comparison.

The structure of the brain then, in addition to the brain's absolute and relative size, has a great deal to do with intelligence. The dolphin has a brain that appears intelligent. Given our present rudimentary state of scientific information about how the higher centers of the brain operate, this less than objective statement is the most we can conscientiously say.

Most of the basic functions for controlling the processes that are necessary for survival in all animals, such as breathing and digestion, are located in the lower portion of the brain called the brain stem. In higher animals this basic brain stem is surrounded by the cerebral cortex. In general, the higher an animal stands on the evolutionary scale the larger its cerebral cortex. It is in the cerebral cortex that the quality we call intelligence is located.

Thus, another possible way of comparing the relative intelligence of man and dolphin would be to find the ratio between the size of the "lower" brain stem and the "higher" cerebral cortex. But here man falls behind both the dolphin and the sperm whale.

The surface of the cerebral cortex of an intelligent animal's brain is deeply marked with ridges, called convolutions. These convolutions increase the surface area of the cortex and in theory provide more cells for intelligent thought. At one time it was popular to compare the well-convoluted brain of a man with the less-convoluted brain of lower animals. But dolphins, and particularly the sperm whale, have brains with more convolutions than the brain of a man.

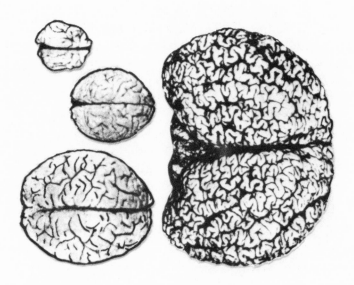

Compare the brain size of the dog, orangutan, human, and sperm whale. Does it seem as if the sperm whale should be more intelligent than man?

Still another method of attacking the problem is to measure the density of the cells in a human brain as compared to the density of the cells in the brains of other animals. First it appeared that the cells in a dolphin's brain were farther apart than those in a man's brain, but later research reversed this finding.

It is quite possible, on the basis of this sort of raw data, to build the case that the dolphin has a better brain than man does and is, potentially at least, more intelligent. A number of scientists and others have attempted to do just that.

But the case for the superiority of dolphin intelligence simply cannot be sustained on physical evidence alone. Scientific study of the structure and function of the brain, human or otherwise, is in its infancy. The brains of dolphins are not just larger and more complex replicas of a man's brain; there are basic structural differences as well, and these may, indeed almost certainly do, have great bearing on the question of intelligence. Basic biochemical differences may also exist in the brains of the different species, about which we yet know nothing. The only fair conclusion we can reach at this stage is that the dolphin appears to have a first-class brain.

Since anatomy is not going to provide any easy answers about dolphin intelligence, we are forced to fall back on the more uncertain business of trying to deduce a creature's intelligence by observing the way it behaves. The problems involved in studying the behavior of apes give some indication of the even more difficult problems men face in trying to study the behavior of dolphins and whales.

Dolphins live in the sea, a region until recently more inaccessible to twentieth-century man than the wildest jungle was to a nineteenth-century explorer. Even today with frogmen, sea labs, and the well-publicized exploits of Jacques Cousteau, we are a long, long way from a detailed picture of the life of wild dolphins. Most dolphins and other whales are nomadic, they roam over vast areas of the sea. Human observers catch only occasional glimpses of them. We are still very much in the position of poor Richard L. Garner trying to study the activities of wild apes while locked inside of his cage that was meant to protect him from "the ferocious beasts of the jungle."

Again we are forced to fall back on the inadequate observation that dolphins *seem* to behave intelligently. The dolphins are social animals who live in large and apparently stable herds. They appear to be quite cooperative and playful, both possible signs of intelligence.

Close-up study of dolphins has become practical only since we have been able to keep them in captivity. Standard aquariums in which fish and other small sea creatures have been displayed simply were not equipped to keep even a small whale. Seals, sea lions, and walruses, which spent much of their time out of the water, had been kept in zoos but whales, according to Lee S. Crandall, former general curator of the Bronx Zoo, have never been considered proper zoological garden subjects.

Smaller whales such as dolphins were first put on display in special facilities like Florida's Marineland and California's Seaquarium. The operators of such facilities soon discovered that dolphins were extremely trainable, and could be turned into first-class attractions. To most people a dolphin is very appealing. Despite their size they are clean-looking and streamlined animals that move through the water with a grace and speed that is quite beautiful to watch. The dolphin's face, though immobile and unexpressive, is frozen into what appears to be a perpetual smile. These animals radiate charm and friendliness, and don't look like the grotesque parodies of human beings monkeys and apes do. One suspects that many people would be less upset at the idea of being closely related to dolphins than to apes.

When such attractive creatures can also be taught to make spectacular leaps out of the water, balance balls on the tips of their beaks, and cavort in a friendly manner with human divers, their appeal becomes irresistible.

The mere fact that dolphins are so trainable indicates some degree of intelligence. But horses and dogs are trainable, too, so this fact alone doesn't tell us much. In order to get some idea of where the dolphin might rank on the scale of relative intelligence it would be necessary to test its performance on some sort of standardized test that could be used with a number of different species. Immediately some important problems arise.

Chimpanzees can be given the same intelligence tests administered to human infants because these tests involve the use of the hands. But dolphins don't have

A trio of dolphins performing a difficult triple-hoop jump at Marineland of Florida. Their movements are perfectly synchronized.

hands, and they cannot be tested by seeing how quickly they learn to put square pegs into square holes and round pegs into round holes. Dolphins could never learn to manipulate locks and keys as chimps do. About the only cross-species test that can be conducted involves a simple Skinner box type of task like learning to push a switch or pull a rope in order to obtain a reward or avoid a punishment. The dolphins could push the switch with their beaks or pull the string with their mouths, and they learned these simple tasks as fast or faster than most apes. But this still doesn't tell us very much.

Problems do arise, as we have seen, in attempting to measure the relative intelligence of man and ape, yet still these two species are quite closely related and, more important, inhabit the same sort of world. Dolphins, being adapted to spending most of their lives under water, are adapted to an entirely different sort of world. The observation that wild chimpanzees are able to make and use simple tools is considered a significant sign of their intelligence. Does the fact that the handless dolphin does not, and could not, make tools mean that it is less intelligent? Can the quality called intelligence be separated from the physical abilities that it may control?

Or from another angle, let us consider the dolphin's sensory world compared to man's and to that of the apes. It has been estimated that man takes in anywhere from 70 to 80 percent of his information about the surrounding world through his eyes. Blindness would be a far greater handicap to a human than deafness. For dolphins the reverse is true.

Dolphins and other whales have eyes, but they are small, and not particularly acute. Dolphins and whales find their way around by sonar, or echo location. Simply described, the dolphin utters a noise, and when this sound strikes a solid object in its path an echo comes back to the dolphin. The dolphin's brain "interprets" the sound and is able to produce a "picture" of the object. A bat navigates in much the same way. The sonar of a dolphin is incredibly sensitive and effective, as repeated tests have shown. A dolphin can detect a tiny ball bearing dropped into the water fifty feet away. Our eyes do not have so great a power of resolution.

The way in which an animal deals with the external world is controlled by the way in which it perceives that world. Thus the dolphin, which perceives the world through sound, probably, indeed almost certainly, "thinks" in a manner very different from men and apes, who perceive the world primarily by visual means.

This very fundamental difference between the sensory worlds of dolphins and men may, at least in part, account for the relatively large size of the dolphin's brain. In their book *Smarter Than Man?* the Swedish scientists Karl-Erik Fichtelius and Sverre Sjölander speculate: "It is probable that dolphins have a well-developed acoustical memory. It could be that acoustical memory requires a greater number of neurons than, say, visual memory. This would mean that a large portion of the dolphin's cerebral cortex consisted of acoustical memory cortex, and that a relatively smaller part would be left over for the other higher mental processes. But about this we know nothing."

So it seems that dolphins are very alien creatures, far more removed from us than the chimpanzee and even the dog. Yet because of their highly developed acoustical equipment, there is one area in which it appears possible that research progress might be made, and that is in the area of language. Most of the spectacular claims about dolphin intelligence made in recent years are based on the presumption that the dolphins possess a complex language. Some people even believe that great progress has already been made in deciphering the "language" of the dolphins and communicating with them.

Dolphins and other whales are social animals. They roam the seas in large packs or herds. Social animals have a need to communicate with one another. Studies of terrestrial social animals show that they do indeed communicate, often in fairly sophisticated ways. Much of this communication can be set down as "instinctive," but the point is that the communication takes place. It is therefore reasonable to assume that the large-brained dolphins also communicate with one another, though our direct evidence in this area is surprisingly and disappointingly scanty.

In recent years scientists armed with new equipment like hydrophones, microphones adapted for detecting underwater sounds, have been able to pick up sounds made by dolphins and whales. Scientists aboard the research vessel *Sea Quest* conducted a study of the California gray whale. The vessel was equipped with hydrophones. As part of the study, the scientists had strung a number of aluminum poles across the entrance to a lagoon frequented by the whales, and by dolphins as well. The first creatures to take notice of the poles were a group of five bottle-nosed dolphins. The hydrophones picked up the whistling noises made by the dolphins. These whistles grew more pronounced as the creatures approached the barrier. Before reaching the poles the group stopped, and one of the dolphins went forward, apparently as a scout. After the scout had swum close to the poles it returned to its companions. There were a few more moments of whistling, and then the dolphins swam on past the poles.

It is appealing to think that the dolphins discussed the matter of the unfamiliar objects in their path, arrived at the rational decision that they were in no danger, and went on their way. But we have no reason to believe that that is what actually happened. Many herd animals use scouts, and their messages are little more than instinctive cries of alarm or danger. A herd of horses, not generally regarded as highly intelligent animals, might have behaved in very much the same way. Extreme caution must be exercised in interpreting stories like this one, particularly since the current popularity of dolphins is so high.

Observations of captive dolphins have produced some evidence of communication. A young dolphin separated from its mother will emit a large number of unusual whistling noises, to which its mother, in a nearby tank, will respond. A dolphin that is ill or injured and having trouble breathing will make sounds that appear to stimulate its companions to try and aid it by raising it to the surface where it can breathe. But again, none of this behavior is entirely unique to dolphins, and it is not necessarily a sign of high intelligence or possession of an advanced language.

In attempting to crack the language of the dolphins, if such a language exists at all, we encounter some truly spectacular difficulties. The problems are due to the dolphin's very complicated and efficient acoustic equipment. Dolphins emit and receive a huge variety of sounds, many of them way beyond the range of normal human hearing. No one was really aware of just how noisy dolphins are until they were tested with equipment that could pick up these high-frequency sounds. While swimming about dolphins are almost continuously making noises of some sort. Most of the sounds, scientists believe, are used in the dolphin's echo location system, and play little part in dolphin-to-dolphin communication. Other sounds, however, seem meant specifically for communication. Problems arise in trying to sort out the different sounds.

Dr. John C. Lilly, who probably did more to bring the dolphin to public attention than any other single individual, tried to teach dolphins how to "speak" in a human fashion. Dolphins can make audible sounds through their blowhole, the nostril on the top of their heads. In some dolphin shows the animals have been taught to "sing," that is, they come to the surface and make strange noises which the promoters label as singing. This stunt strikes one as being on a par with the "singing" dogs that used to be familiar vaudeville attractions. At first glance dolphins appear even less promising subjects for learning human speech than do apes. But Dr. Lilly thought that his dolphins were actually trying to mimic human speech.

Dr. Lilly amplified the sounds made by some of his

captive dolphins. He found that on one occasion a dolphin seemed to be making sounds that resembled human laughter. There had been some laughing going on near the dolphin's tank shortly before the recording was made. Somewhat later he made an unexpected discovery. In his book *Man and Dolphin* Dr. Lilly says, "We discovered that (in a very terse shorthand and quacking sort of way) this dolphin had been mimicking some of the things I had been saying."

But parrots and mynah birds do a much better job of mimicking human speech without having the faintest notion of the meaning behind the words they are using, so mimicry is not in itself a sign of intelligence.

Dr. Lilly reported one genuinely eerie experience with dolphin "speech." One particular dolphin (named Lizzie) in his research center was thought to be very talented at mimicry. The dolphin became ill, a development that genuinely saddened the scientist, who was very fond of the animal. Shortly before she died a tape recorder picked up noises from Lizzie which to Dr. Lilly sounded like the dolphin saying, "This is a trick," with a particular hissing accent.

Were these the "last words" of a dying dolphin? We cannot be sure. Some who have heard the recording think the dolphin said: "It's six o'clock!" a phrase that had been uttered loudly near the dolphin's tank shortly before the recording was made. Others hear no meaning at all in the dolphin's noises.

From time to time newspapers and popular magazines carry accounts of scientists and nonscientists who say that they have discovered the secret of the language of the dolphins. Generally these claims come from individuals who believe that they have discerned a pattern in greatly amplified and speeded up or slowed down recordings of dolphin sounds. But most outsiders who have listened to such recordings hear nothing but a succession of apparently meaningless noises. At present, the case for a dolphin language awaits more substantial proof.

As far back as 1900, ape enthusiast Richard L. Garner was sure that he had discovered an elaborate chimpanzee language. Our study of the language and intelligence of the dolphins now stands about where the study of chimpanzee language and intelligence stood at the end of the nineteenth century. There is still much to learn. We are only now beginning to get some accurate idea of the structure of ape communication and to make some educated guesses as to ape intelligence. With dolphins the experimental program will be infinitely more difficult because the dolphin is such an alien creature, and words like intelligence and language may have to be considerably redefined in order to fit them.

But the dolphin isn't the only member of the whale family that may possess a high order of intelligence; it is only the one which has been most accessible to study so far. Another good candidate for intelligence honors is the killer whale. This much maligned creature is a larger version of the dolphin. Instead of being strictly a fish-eater, as is the dolphin, the killer whale is adapted for killing and eating larger sea creatures like seals, dolphins, and even some of the giant whales. It has—or had until quite recently—the reputation for being a vicious and lustful killer, which not only attacked whales, often for the sheer pleasure of killing, but attacked men whenever it got a chance. There were stories of killer whales trying to ram small boats and of knocking stranded polar explorers off of ice floes. It was the case of the gorilla all over again although, admittedly, the killer whale is a very efficient sea-going hunter and the gorilla a peaceful plant-eater.

But over the past decade a few killer whales have been captured and observed in captivity. Killer whales hadn't previously survived for very long in captivity because they were either injured or ill when captured (which is how they were captured) and because facilities for keeping so large an animal—they may reach a length of about thirty feet—were inadequate. It turned out that in captivity these ferocious killers were just about as friendly and affectionate to the humans who cared for them as their smaller relatives, the dolphins, had been. Kandu, a killer whale kept at the Seattle Marine Aquarium, was such a popular attraction that it became sort of an unofficial symbol for the city itself. Tales of the behavior of killer whales at least suggest that they are not only intelligent creatures but possess a fairly sophisticated means of communication.

The nearly extinct humpback whale has been the object of several years of study by Dr. Roger S. Payne of Rockefeller University. Dr. Payne's work attracted a great deal of attention when he announced that the humpback whale sings. The song of the humpback whale is really a series of low, rumbling noises, punctuated with rising trumpetlike blasts. The sounds may go on anywhere from a few seconds to a few minutes. Recordings of the humpback whale "songs," along with musical pieces they have inspired, became popular records.

Dr. Payne believes that what he called songs are probably some form of communication among humpback whales. Each whale seems to have a very different and characteristic series of noises, and it is Dr. Payne's theory that the individual "songs" may be used for identification purposes.

One intriguing bit of information turned up in Dr. Payne's research was that the humpback whale songs were detected at a depth of 3300 feet off the coast of North America. At this depth two sound-reflecting layers exist close together. Dr. Payne explains: "This is a layer of water that, for various reasons—temperature, density, and so forth—has acoustical qualities which permit the transmission of sound over very long distances, in some cases more than a thousand miles. I'm not saying that whales sit on two sides of the ocean and chat with each other, but it's possible that they produce sounds either in or out of the sound channel, which may allow them to flock together. This could take the simple form of 'Humpback whale here!' or maybe even a more sophisticated 'George here!' "

Finally there is the great sperm whale. No one who discusses the problem of intelligence can possibly ignore the creature that has the largest and possibly most complex brain ever known. One might, I suppose, make the case that the sperm whale is really a stupid creature, because man has been able to hunt it very nearly to extinction. But just because these huge animals have not proved themselves to be very good at escaping man's powered boats and harpoons is not necessarily a sign of lack of intelligence. If mere survival were an accurate measure of intelligence then the rat and the cockroach would have to rank next to man on the intelligence scale.

Though we have learned a good deal about how to kill large whales we know depressingly little else about them. And because of their great size it seems highly unlikely that we are going to be able to keep captive sperm whales in the near future.

The primary food of the sperm whale is the squid. In pursuit of its prey the sperm whale is known to dive several thousand feet. There in the inky and icy blackness of the deep sea the sperm whale depends on its highly efficient sonar to locate its food. The sperm whale appears to have the most complex acoustical equipment of all the whales, and its adaptation for life in the abyss may also make it the most alien of all the whales.

All we know for sure about sperm whale communication is that they do communicate, for scientists have recorded sperm whale noises, and whalers have often noticed how an attack on one whale will alert all the others in the vicinity even if they did not witness the attack.

Beyond this evidence we must rely on anecdotes that seem to indicate sperm whale intelligence and communication. A striking story appeared in "The Cruise of the Cachalot" by Frank T. Bullen, first published in 1897. *The Cachalot* was a whaling ship, and when this incident occurred the ship's hold and deck were already completely filled with whale products and it would have been pointless to kill any more whales. The author believed that the school of whales began "disporting all around the ship apparently conscious of our helplessness to interfere with them."

Bullen goes on to say: "The whole school surrounded the ship, and performed some of the strangest evolutions imaginable. As if instigated by one common impulse, they all elevated their massive heads above the surface of the sea, and remained for some time in that position, solemnly bobbing up and down amid the glittering wavelets like movable boulders of black rock. Then, all suddenly reversed themselves, and, elevating their broad flukes in the air, commenced to beat them slowly and rhythmically upon the water, like so many machines. Being almost a perfect calm, every movement of the great mammals could be plainly seen; some of them even passed so near to us that we could see how the lower jaw hung down, while the animal was swimming in a normal position."

The purpose of this strange ritual, if that indeed is what it was, is quite unknown. Since we have nearly driven these magnificent animals to extinction it is unlikely that anyone will ever see the likes of this spectacle again.

Dr. John C. Lilly becomes quite humble when speaking of the sperm whale in his book *The Mind of the Dolphin*. Lilly says: "Before they are annihilated by man, I would like to exchange ideas with a sperm whale. I am not sure that they would be interested in communicating with me because my brain obviously is so much more limited than theirs. Somehow, I am sure that their huge brain is used effectively. I am also sure that it has capacities beyond my present comprehension."

Most scientists who have studied the intelligence of dolphins and whales feel that statements like that are sheer romantic fantasies. Scientists commonly rank the dolphin somewhere between the chimpanzee and the dog in intelligence, not a very exalted position considering all of the publicity that has surrounded them.

The argument over the intelligence of the dolphins and whales compared with that of apes and men will continue for a long time, and perhaps it will never really be resolved. All the publicity has had one good result—it has made us more whale conscious, and probably helped to spur efforts to preserve the world's badly depleted whale stock.

It has also had one negative effect—the U.S. Navy, and presumably other navies as well, are now training dolphins and other small whales in the hope that they can be used for various tasks in warfare, including carrying underwater bombs. It is doubtful that the trained dolphin, no matter how intelligent it might turn out to be, will revolutionize sea warfare, as the trained horse revolutionized land warfare centuries ago. But the fact that we are even attempting to use dolphins in the military at all is just another ominous indication of mankind's capacity to turn the most harmless bits of knowledge to destructive purposes.

Whatever final conclusions we may reach about the intelligence of dolphins, whales, apes, or any other animals, the result is not likely to touch most of our lives directly. But the problem of measuring and rating human intelligence is one which affects every one of us, and it is to this problem that we now turn.

The killer whale is a large dolphin known for its ferocity, but few people know that it is also among the most intelligent of mammals.

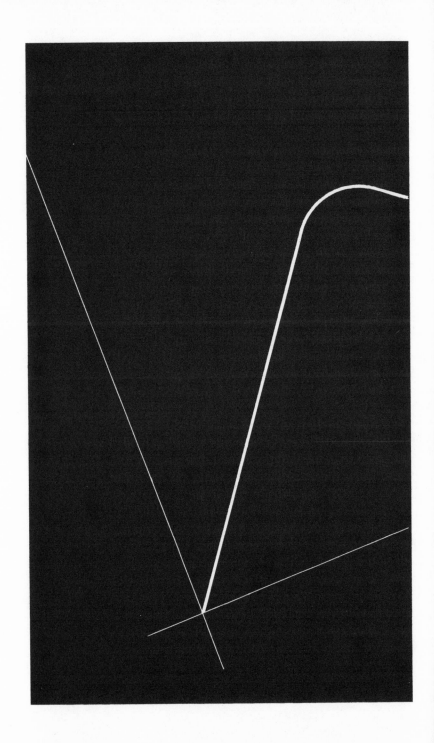

5

The Rise and Partial Fall of the I.Q. Test

The idea that human intelligence could or should be tested really began with the nineteenth-century British scientist Sir Francis Galton. Galton was a Victorian gentleman with enough money and leisure time to pursue his wide-ranging and occasionally odd interests wherever they led. He was a man possessed of a highly original and fertile mind, a tremendous amount of energy, and robust good health; he lived to be nearly ninety. Before he died in 1911 Galton had accomplished enough to do credit to the lives of three ordinary men.

Galton was trained as a physician, but upon his graduation from Cambridge he went off to Africa like many another adventurous English gentleman, and spent years traveling around "the dark continent." As a result of his travels he produced a number of excellent books filled with what he considered useful advice for the traveler in Africa. For example, Galton suggests, when faced with a charging lion: ". . . keep cool and watchful, and your chance of escape is far greater than a non-sportsman would imagine."

After his African adventures Galton turned his attention and energy to the study of meterology. In a few years of concentrated effort he had laid the foundations for the modern science of weather-mapping.

But Galton is not remembered for his travel books or his weather maps. He did his most important work after 1859. In that year Charles Darwin, who also happened to be Galton's cousin, published his epic-making book on evolution, *The Origin of Species.* Galton, like most other scientists of the time, felt the pull of the newly glamorous biological sciences. He spent the rest of his life working on biological problems, particularly the problems of human heredity. To Galton it appeared as though his cousin had not only found the origin of the animal species, but also the origin of the differences between individual members of the human species.

One of Galton's most memorable contributions was the concept of eugenics. Eugenics holds that the human race can be improved by selective breeding. It seemed absurd to a tidy-minded man like Francis Galton that dogs and cattle were being bred along scientifically established principles, but human beings engaged in indiscriminate breeding. His theory aroused a great deal of interest, and eugenics societies of one sort or another were founded throughout the Western world. But eugenics was a theory more talked about than practiced.

Unfortunately Galton's eugenics ideas did contribute, at least indirectly, to one of the most horrifying episodes in modern history. Some of the followers of Adolf Hitler used the excuse of racial improvement along eugenic lines to justify their attempt to exterminate whole sections of the human race. Since the end of World War II eugenics has had a bad name. What happened to the eugenics idea in the hands of the Nazis provides a ghastly example of what can happen when an honest but unsubstantiated theory gets into the hands of vicious and stupid men. Still, Galton cannot really be blamed for the Nazi death camps. He wanted to improve the human race, not exterminate a part of it.

Galton's thought was that to improve the human breed, human characteristics, mental and physical, had to be classified and carefully examined. He tried a great number of systems in his attempt to organize human diversity. He even tried to relate various individual differences to fingerprints and, in the process, worked out a thorough fingerprint classification system. It was largely through Galton's work that the use of fingerprints later became so important in criminal investigation.

Galton collected much of his data on human diversity at his Anthropometric Laboratory in the South Kensington Museum in London. It was a strange sort of laboratory: a long, narrow room with a table full of scientific apparatus. Visitors filing through the room could learn their height, weight, breathing power, strength on certain standard tests, and a number of other interesting things about themselves. For the privilege the visitors paid threepence each. "Galton was thus perhaps the only psychologist to have his subjects pay him, rather than the more usual arrangement," remarked a modern psychologist a bit wistfully.

The "psychological" tests Galton conducted at his Anthropometric Laboratory would hardly be considered psychological today. Many of them involved determining such things as how high a sound a subject could hear, or how well a subject could discriminate between tints of different colored wools. The reason Galton used tests of this sort was that he believed that since knowledge comes through the senses, those individuals with the keenest senses should also have the keenest minds. This sensory view of intelligence was not very influential, but some of Galton's other ideas about intelligence were.

Up until Galton's time the general attitude about intelligence was that the human race consisted of a tiny number of geniuses, and a tiny number of idiots. The vast majority of men were equally endowed with mental powers. Whatever they achieved was primarily the result of hard work and willpower. For Victorian Englishmen it was a comfortable view, for it appeared as though the wealthy and successful really deserved their wealth and success. Galton, however, saw mental traits as based upon physical factors, and he arrived at very different conclusions about intelligence. Intelligence, he thought, could be inherited just as hair color or blood type could be inherited.

Galton's thinking on this point had been influenced by the work of a Belgian statistician named Lambert Adolphe Jacques Quetelet. Quetelet was the first to apply statistical methods to the study of human characteristics. After collecting statistics on a large variety of human measurements he discovered that they fell into what came to be called a normal distribution. If, for example, the characteristic in question was the height of individuals in a particular area, Quetelet noticed that there would be a few extremely tall people, and a few extremely short people. The bulk of individuals would be found between these two extremes, with the numbers falling off sharply as one approached the extremes. If the data about height was plotted on a chart, the result would be a curve shaped roughly like a bell.

If physical characteristics had a normal distribution, Galton reasoned, then mental characteristics must fall into the same sort of distribution. This meant that in addition to a few geniuses and a few idiots there were also measurable differences in mental ability for the mass of people between these extremes. People could be more or less intelligent, just as they were taller and shorter, without having to be either giants or midgets.

What accounted for these differences? The result of Galton's thinking and research on this problem was a book called *Hereditary Genius*. This was the first scientific investigation of what we call intelligence, and one that has influenced, in both subtle and overt ways, most thinking about intelligence ever since.

In the preface to his book Galton wrote: "The idea of investigating the subject of hereditary genius occurred to me during the course of a purely ethnological enquiry into the mental peculiarities of different races, when the fact that characteristics cling to families was so frequently forced upon my notice."

Taking the *Dictionary of Men of Our Time* for 1865 (a sort of nineteenth-century *Who's Who*) and the obituaries of prominent persons in the London *Times* for the year 1868, Galton picked out all those he classed as "eminent" in a variety of fields, and studied their family trees. He discovered that leaders in any one field—politics, the church, science, etc.—tended to be related to others who had held similar positions. Galton's own pedigree seemed to bear out his theory that mental characteristics were determined mainly by heredity. Galton's grandfather was Erasmus Darwin, a physician and scientific philosopher of some importance. Erasmus Darwin had also been the grandfather, by another wife, of Charles Darwin. It appeared more than plausible that the scientifically inquiring mind of grandfather Erasmus had been passed on, by heredity, to his two famous grandsons.

Galton took little heed of such things as family tradition and social advantage. According to his theories of heredity, if a man succeeded in a field, as had his father or grandfather before him, it was because he had inherited the mental abilities that made him succeed, not because his family position gave him advantages denied others. In the endless argument over what influences men's lives—heredity or environment—Francis Galton came down firmly on the side of heredity.

We can see now that Galton's tests of mental abilities were pitifully incomplete by modern standards. His statistics were crude and misguided. In fact, Galton's faith in measurement often passed beyond the bounds of the reasonable. Once he tried to map the distribution of good looks in England, and another time he attempted to chart the efficacy of prayer by statistical methods.

Also, Galton's theories on heredity were severely handicapped by his lack of knowledge of how heredity worked. The basis for all modern studies of heredity was laid by Gregor Mendel, an Austrian monk whose work was virtually unknown until rediscovered by Hugo de Vries in 1900. By that time Galton was eighty and past being able to make any basic alterations in his thinking.

In the light of twentieth-century knowledge it is easy to ridicule many of Galton's nineteenth-century misconceptions. His reputation has also suffered because he was less brilliant and less cautious than his cousin, Charles Darwin. But Galton was not unimportant in the history of science; indeed in the field of behavioral science it would be hard to overestimate his importance. Galton really began the controversy between heredity versus environment as the major determining factor of intelligence—a controversy which is hotter than ever today.

The testing of mental abilities begun at the Anthropometric Laboratory continues, in one form or another, to this day, a century after people first began filing past Galton's strange testing apparatus and plunking down threepence to see how they scored. Unlike Galton's subjects, we are nowadays often tested whether we want to be or not, and the results of the tests may have profound effects upon our future.

An American student of Galton's, James McKeen Cattell, brought the idea of mental testing to the United States. In the 1890s Cattell's work stimulated a brief but intense flurry of interest in mental testing in America. He tried tests modeled on Galton's on a large number of students, and advocated that similar tests be given in all schools. A serious problem, however, was that people who scored well on the Galton-type tests did not necessarily do well in schoolwork. Doing well in school was considered the primary practical expression of high mental ability, and so the Galton-modeled sensory tests were largely abandoned as measures of intelligence.

The basic form for most modern-day intelligence tests comes from the work of the French psychologist Alfred Binet. Binet worked primarily with children in a little laboratory that he had set up in a Paris public school on the Rue de la Grange-Aux-Belles. Like Galton, Binet was a passionate tester and measurer. He measured head size and lung capacity, tested eyesight and hearing, and a myriad other physical characteristics of the Paris schoolchildren.

The diversity in the children fascinated him and, like Galton, he looked for some way to classify and understand these differences. One popular theory of the time was that there was a relationship between certain physical characteristics, particularly the shape of the ear, and the character and intelligence of an individual. Pictures of parts of faces lined the walls of one of the rooms in Binet's laboratory, pictures of ears being the most common. Fingerprints too were investigated in the Binet laboratory. It was even said that on occasion Binet employed the services of a Persian palm reader.

Binet's intelligence tests grew out of his trial-and-error method of testing. Working with the normal children in his school and with a group of retarded children at a nearby hospital, Binet tried out certain types of tasks that might be performed by normal children of a certain age, but not by the retarded. The aim was to find out what was "normal" or "average."

Binet wrote: "What my assistants and I set ourselves to find out, in a strictly scientific manner, was the physical and mental value of the average child at various ages.

Once having discovered this, we drew up tables of averages. We are able, for instance, to say: 'This boy's growth is retarded. Though twelve years of age, he has only the development of a child of nine. He will require special attention and special nourishment. This other scholar, on the contrary, is physically in advance of his age. He is more muscular, taller and stronger than a boy of ten.' A third boy, we note, shows a remarkable mastery over himself, while a fourth is emotional and nervous. One is an observer, calm and calculating; the other imaginative. If the most is to be made out of them in later life, they must be educated differently."

Binet's work came to the attention of the Paris educational authorities. They asked him to devise a test that could be used to separate normal children, who could enter the regular school system, from dull children, who would not benefit from standard education, but needed special instruction. The French scientist held no particular theory about innate intelligence, or even about how children learn. He simply faced up to the practical problems of trying to construct a test that would predict how well, or poorly, any particular student would do in the Paris school system at the turn of the century.

Through trial and error, Binet came up with a graduated series of tasks, stunts he often called them, starting with those that could be performed by a very young child, and ranging upward in difficulty. The following are some examples from the original Binet intelligence test:

Age Three
Point to your nose; your eyes; your mouth.

Age Four
Are you a boy or a girl?

Age Five
Copy this square.

Age Six
What is a fork? a table? a horse? a mama?

Age Seven
What is missing in this picture? (Drawing of a woman's face with no mouth.)

Age Eight
What is the difference between wood and glass?

Age Nine
Same as question for age six, but better definition needed: for example, no credit would be given for, "A fork is to eat with."

Age Ten
Make a sentence using the words, *Paris, fortune, gutter.*

There was, of course, a great deal more to the test, and Binet was constantly checking questions, dropping some, adding new ones, and moving items from one age group to another. But the standard form of the Binet intelligence test has never really changed. The examiner would begin by asking a child those questions corresponding to his chronological age, or a bit below. The tester then continued with questions at a higher age level. The "mental age" of the child was determined by the highest group of tests he could pass. Additional credit was given for giving proper responses on different items in higher age groups on the test.

The idea that a fairly simple and easily administered test could determine someone's "mental age" became enormously popular. But just before World War I a German psychologist named Wilhelm Stern suggested that there was a better way of expressing the results of the Binet tests than by determining a mental age. Stern figured test results by finding the ratio between the subject's chronological age and his mental age as shown on the test.

Ratios can be very revealing. For example, it would not be a terribly big jump if a ten-year-old tested one year ahead of his chronological age. But if a five-year-old tested a year ahead this would be far more significant.

The formula for arriving at the ratio was simple. The mental age was divided by the chronological age, and the result multiplied by one hundred to get rid of the decimal point. In the case of the ten-year-old who had successfully tested out at an eleven-year-old level, the result of the formula would give him a score of 110. For the five-year-old who had tested out at a six-year-old level, the score would be 120. Whereas both had scored one year ahead of their chronological ages, the ratio for the five-year-old was greater, and thus his score was larger.

An American psychologist named Lewis Terman coined the term *intelligence quotient* to designate the score on a Binet test. Since then the abbreviation I.Q. has become a familiar part of our language. The center point on a graph of I.Q. scores is 100. Anyone with an I.Q. score above 100 is considered above average, anyone with an I.Q. score below 100, below average. Today most I.Q. tests are no longer scored by obtaining the ratio of the chronological age to the mental age. But the scores are still converted into numbers where the average is 100, and they are still called I.Q.s, though strictly speaking they are not quotients any more.

But what is the I.Q.? Does it represent some innate and unchanging mental quality that we can call intelligence? Binet certainly didn't think so. As early as 1909 he made known his disagreement with some of the inferences being drawn from the results of his tests. ". . .

Some recent philosophers appear to have given their moral support to the deplorable verdict that the intelligence of an individual is a fixed quantity. . . . We must protest and act against this brutal pessimism."

Wilhelm Stern didn't think that the I.Q. score represented a fixed inborn quantity either. He wrote in 1914: "No series of tests, however skillfully selected it may be, does reach the innate intellectual endowment, stripped of all complications, but rather this endowment in conjunction with all influences to which the examinee has been subjected up to the moment of testing."

But somehow the cautious reservations of these two pioneers of intelligence testing did not make much of an impression in America. The I.Q. tests were accepted more enthusiastically in America than they had been in Europe, and the results given greater weight than anywhere else in the world. In 1916 a Binet test was administered in a Wyoming courtroom to a prisoner on trial for murder. The prisoner fared so poorly on the test that the jury acquitted him by reason of his mental condition. Throughout the country tests were given to men in prisons and the results seemed to show that those behind bars were mentally far below normal. These results fitted neatly with the preconceived notion that there was a subnormal criminal class. In 1914 a magazine commented: "The Binet tests are all the rage."

The greatest spurt in I.Q. testing in America came in 1917 when America entered the First World War. Binet's original tests had been designed to be administered to children on an individual basis. But the U.S. Army was faced with a mass problem. Huge numbers of raw draftees from all parts of the country and from all walks of life were entering the service. From this mass of unfamiliar humanity commanders wanted to find out quickly which men should be sent to officers' training school, and which should be mustered out as unfit for duty, put in labor battalions, or given some sort of special training.

The Army didn't have the time or personnel to administer individual tests to each draftee. What was needed was a test that could be given to a large number of men by officers who had no special training in psychological testing. The Army put together a committee of seven leading psychologists to devise a mass intelligence test. The chairman of the committee was Robert Yerkes, whose reputation was based on his studies of animal behavior. Yerkes later admitted he was chosen simply because he was president of the American Psychological Association that year. Others on the committee, such as Lewis Terman, however, had worked extensively with the Binet tests.

It so happened that Terman's pupil, Arthur Otis, had already been constructing a group intelligence test when the Army decided it needed one. By and large, the committee adopted the material Otis had already prepared. In six weeks the tests were ready for the printers, and a few weeks after that there was a trial run with four thousand men. By the beginning of 1919, nearly two million men had taken the Army intelligence tests.

In practice the Army found that it needed two different types of tests—which they labeled Alpha and Beta. The Alpha tests were the standard Binet type, with printed instructions. The Beta tests were designed to be administered to men who could not read, or sometimes even speak, English. A large number of those the Army inducted in World War I were either illiterate or non-English-speaking. The directions for the Beta tests were given mostly in pantomime. An officer would stand in the front of the test room at a blackboard that had the same figures on it that were on the printed test blanks. By tapping with a pointer, motions of the hands, and other signals, the officer tried to convey what the men were supposed to do on the paper.

The Beta tests also differed from the Alpha tests in substance. The Alpha depended heavily on English verbal skills, while the Beta examinations used tests such as matching columns of digits and completing incomplete pictures. In general the Beta tests were considered much less successful than the Alpha, because the technique of nonlanguage intelligence testing was new and untried at the time.

The purpose of all of these tests, according to the Secretary of the Army, was ". . . to measure native intelligence and ability, not schooling; to disclose what a man can do with his head and hands, not what he has learned from books. . . ."

The idea that the Army tests were "scientific"—meaning foolproof and absolutely reliable measures of some important identifiable quantity called "intelligence" —was soon communicated to the public at large. Typical of what people were being told about intelligence tests was an article "How High Do You Stand on the Rating Scale?" that appeared in *The American Magazine* in March 1919. Part of the article concerned a fictitious Lieutenant Ralph Jones:

"There is no divergence of opinion concerning Ralph among the army officials in Washington. They do not guess about him; they do not classify him with any such vague terms as 'good' or 'mediocre' or 'poor.' They know precisely where he stands in relation to every other officer of similar rank in the army. By scientific tests they have measured his mind and rated his abilities. . . .

"How has the army in so short a time arrived at so precise an estimate of Lieutenant Jones' capacities? How is it possible for his military employers to agree so exactly concerning him, when his employers in civil life were so far apart? The answers to those questions are very important to any man who expects either to be an applicant for a position or to pass upon the applications of other men

Test Yourself

Sample Army Test, March 1919 issue,
The American Magazine

With your pencil make a dot over any one of these letters
F G H I J, and a comma after the longest of these three words:
boy mother girl. Then, if Christmas comes in March, make a
cross right here....but if not, pass along to the next question,
and tell where the sun rises....If you believe that Edison
discovered America, cross out what you just wrote, but if it
was someone else, put in a number to complete this sentence:
"A horse has...feet." Write yes, no matter whether China is in
Africa or not....; and then give a wrong answer to this
question: "How many days are there in the week?"...Write
any letter except g just after this comma,   and then write no if
2 times 5 are 10....Now, if Tuesday comes after Monday, make
two crosses here....; but if not, make a circle here....or else
a square here....Be sure to make three crosses between these
two names of boys: George....Henry. Notice these two numbers: 3, 5. If iron is heavier than water, write the larger number
here..., but if iron is lighter write the smaller number here....
Show by a cross when the nights are longer; in summer?...in
winter?...Give the correct answer to this question: "Does
water run uphill?"...and repeat your answer here....Do
nothing here (5+7=....), unless you skipped the preceding
question; but write the first letter of your first name and the
last letter of your last name at the end of this line:....

This test takes the average adult 125 seconds. If people were divided into Excellent,
Good, Fair, and Poor, Excellent is 100 seconds or less; 100 to 125 seconds is Good;
125 to 150 is Fair; and anything over 150
seconds is Poor.

in the next few years. They constitute one of the big contributions which are to be made to the future of business by the world war."

The Army scores were not expressed in the now familiar I.Q. rankings but rather on a total of points awarded for correct answers. On the basis of these points men were divided into classes, ranked from A to E. The lowest group, the Es, about one half of one percent, were discharged. Otherwise the use made of the scores varied from base to base, depending on the inclinations of any particular commanding officer. In some camps As and Bs were lumped together in units. The Cs also had their own units, while Ds might wind up in labor battalions and assigned only menial work, or given special training to see if they could be of greater use to the Army.

After the war, the tests provided a nasty shock for the American public. The results were released, and the point scores and grades, which didn't mean much to people outside of professional psychological circles, were translated into mental age levels, figures the public could easily grasp. According to the tests, the average Army draftee of World War I had a mental age level of fourteen years.

The showing of the average draftee wasn't as bad as it first appeared, because the scale stopped at a mental age of fifteen. Every score above that was considered within the normal adult range of intelligence. So the average draftee had tested out only one year below normal adult level. More significantly, though, the tests had been hurriedly constructed and administered under wartime conditions. Even the staunchest defenders of intelligence testing had to admit that the scores were at least partly influenced by the subject's educational background. College graduates, for example, consistently scored much higher than those with less schooling. Fourteen was the average age of a high school freshman, but many of those drafted had never even completed elementary school.

There were other bugs in the test as well. For example, women averaged ten points lower than men on the tests. Hardly a surprising result when the test contained such questions as: Where is the Packard Automobile Company's plant located?—a bit of information men at that time would be far more likely to know than women, but hardly one that would have any bearing on general intelligence.

Yet for all their acknowledged shortcomings, the Army tests had given intelligence measuring a respectability bordering upon awe. As predicted in *The American Magazine* article many companies began testing programs to determine who would be hired, promoted, and transferred. The greatest market for intelligence tests was the schools. In the years following World War I practically every school system in the country began some sort of intelligence scoring program.

A huge testing industry grew up to meet the demand. The tests were constantly being checked, refined, and revised. A wide variety of different types of tests were issued. Psychologists and professional testers continually issued warnings about how the tests should be administered and interpreted. Yet the basic assumption—that I.Q. tests measured some distinct, innate, and extremely important mental quality—was never really questioned.

Secrecy added to the aura of infallibility that surrounded intelligence tests. A person might be refused a job or promotion because his test score was too low (or in some cases too high). Yet often the score, or even the reason for the applicant's rejection, was not revealed. I.Q. scores became a permanent part of a child's school record. The score might be made known to other teachers, college administrators, even prospective employers, but often not to the child himself or to his parents. At best the parent might get an "interpretation" of a child's score by a school official who might or might not be qualified to make such an interpretation.

Not long after widespread I.Q. testing began some people began to fear that it had become a Frankenstein's monster. As early as 1922, columnist and social commentator Walter Lippmann was thoroughly alarmed by the claims made by proponents of I.Q. tests. He wrote in the Nov. 15, 1922 issue of the *New Republic* magazine: "They claim not only that they are really measuring intelligence, but that intelligence is innate, hereditary, and predetermined. . . . Intelligence testing in the hands of men who hold this dogma could not but lead to an intellectual caste system. . . ."

What bothered Lippmann was not the tests themselves, which might be useful tools, but the belief that they were infallible. He wrote: "If, for example, the impression takes root that these tests really measure intelligence, that they reveal 'scientifically' his [the child's] predestined ability, then it would be a thousand times better if all the intelligence testers and all their questionnaires were sunk without warning into the Sargasso Sea. One only has to read around in the literature of the subject . . . to see how easily the intelligence test can be turned into an engine of cruelty, how easily in the hands of blundering or prejudiced men it could turn into a method of stamping a permanent sense of inferiority upon the soul of a child. . . .

"I do not mean to say that the intelligence test is certain to be abused. I do mean to say it lends itself so easily to abuse that the temptation will be enormous. . . . For the whole drift of the propaganda based on intelligence testing is to treat people with low intelligence quotients as congenitally and hopelessly inferior."

Professional testers like Lewis Terman responded by acknowledging that abusing the tests was possible, "but they simply aren't. That is one of the recognized rules of the game." In general, philosophical objections like those raised by Walter Lippmann made little dent in the burgeoning intelligence testing industry, as more and more tests were administered to more and more people.

The worst fears concerning the abuse of intelligence testing turned out to be groundless, and an intellectual caste system based on I.Q. never developed in America. While some employers and schools laid great stress on the tests, others did not. In general, the impact of the tests on the lives of individuals was far less than one might have expected. As often as not test results were simply filed and forgotten. But for decades there was no serious widespread attack on the use of I.Q. tests.

It wasn't until the 1960s that I.Q. tests began to face important challenges on several fronts. Some education departments had broken tradition and allowed parents to see their children's I.Q. test scores. But in 1961, a Long Island, New York, high school refused to allow Edward Van Allen to see his son's records; when he sued them, the New York State Supreme Court decided the case in his favor.

In 1964 the New York City Board of Education did away with I.Q. testing entirely. Other boards of education followed suit, though often reluctantly.

The I.Q. test was in court again in 1971 when a group of Mexican-Americans sued the California State Board of Education because of alleged abuses of the test. The following year the California state legislature abolished mandatory statewide group I.Q. testing, and prohibited any I.Q. testing of children from non-English-speaking countries until they have resided in the United States at least two years.

Not only school testing was under attack. In 1971 the United States Supreme Court ruled unanimously against a company that was using general intelligence tests as a basis for promotion in jobs which required manual skills. The court held that any test for promotion must relate directly to the skills needed on the job in question.

These decisions were rendered against group intelligence tests, which had already been slightly suspect anyway. But even the individually administered tests were losing out in court. In 1972 a federal court in Philadelphia ruled that I.Q. test scores could no longer be used as a reason for not providing education for all mentally retarded children. Traditionally mentally retarded children were carefully tested, and those who scored below a certain level classed as uneducable and untrainable. Such children received no education whatsoever, on the theory that according to I.Q. tests, education would be a waste of time and money. A group acting on behalf of these retarded children sued and won. I.Q. tests in Pennsylvania could no longer be used as a reason for refusing any child education. The governor of Pennsylvania hailed the decision by saying the court had "recognized the relative ineffectiveness of I.Q. tests as a gauge of the development potential of a retarded child."

Though the I.Q. test in its many forms is no longer considered infallible or sacred in education or business, intelligence testing has by no means been abandoned, or is it about to be abandoned. Millions are still tested every year. The results of these tests are still used in hiring and promotion, in placing students in different classes in school, and they are even taken into account in setting long-term goals for our entire society. Rightly or wrongly the I.Q. continues to exert a powerful influence on how we think of others, and of ourselves.

In the following chapter we will take a closer look at how modern I.Q. tests are constructed and scored.

6

What Do
I.Q. Tests Test?

While some of the mystery and prestige of I.Q. tests has been stripped away in recent years, most of us still identify I.Q., that score obtained on a standard intelligence test, with a very important quality of mind called intelligence.

An international group called the Mensa Society is supposed to consist solely of highly intelligent people— that is, people who score in the top three percent on intelligence tests. However, in the late 1960s, Mensa ran into some problems. Roughly three out of four of the prospective members selected on one kind of intelligence test failed to be selected by a second test, and three out of four of those chosen by the second type of test could not meet the standards of the first test.

Obviously human intelligence is not an easy thing to pin down. In an article entitled "Five Myths About Your IQ" that appeared in the *Atlantic Monthly* Professor Christopher Jencks of Harvard and Mary Jo Bane observe: "It includes all mental abilities required to solve whatever theoretical or practical problems they happen to think important. At one moment intelligence is the ability to unravel French syntax. At another it is the intuition required to understand what ails a neurotic friend. At still another it is the capacity to anticipate future demand for hog bristles. We know from experience that those skills are only loosely related to one another. People who are 'intelligent' in one context often are remarkably 'stupid' in another."

A classic example is Albert Einstein. As a youth the great physicist was a mediocre student and was asked to leave school. He failed his entrance examinations to the Polytechnic in Zurich, Switzerland, and had his doctoral thesis rejected at the University of Zurich. When he finally graduated he had a hard time finding a job. Even after he became world-famous Einstein was known as a remarkably impractical man. Occasionally he was said to forget to cash checks, and use them as bookmarks instead. Yet Einstein, whose name is virtually synonymous with genius, could hardly be called unintelligent.

An even more striking case is that of Jan Masaryk, who was for a time head of the government of Czechoslovakia. During a childhood stay in America Masaryk was briefly confined to an institution for the mentally retarded because of his poor performance on an intelligence test.

Since there are many different qualities that might be called intelligence, what is it that intelligence tests are supposed to measure?

Psychologists have given a large and confusing variety of answers to this question. They range from the ability "to judge well, comprehend well, reason well," to the ability "to carry on abstract thinking," to "innate, general, cognitive (thinking) ability." Some psychologists hold that intelligence tests probe a single general intelligence factor, often called "the G factor." Others say that there are really two or more kinds of basic intelligence. An incident typical of the controversy surrounding this subject occurred in 1959. A leading psychologist wrote a long paper defining intelligence. But his critics noted wickedly that he had to spend most of his time defining definition.

Even among those who compile intelligence tests there is no general agreement about what they are testing for. The testers most often dismiss the question of what is intelligence as a meaningless one. They say that intelligence is what intelligence tests measure. Perhaps more an evasion than an answer, but since no one knows what intelligence really is, this statement has become one of the most frequently repeated descriptions of intelligence.

How is it possible to construct a test for an unknown quantity? How can anyone know the tests are working properly? And what possible meaning could the results of such a test have? Alfred Binet, the French psychologist whose work founded modern intelligence testing, had no particular theory about intelligence or learning. He faced the practical problem of constructing a test that would predict which students would succeed in the public schools of the time and which would not. In making up his test Binet found tasks or problems that most Parisian schoolchildren of a particular age could do. He set up a hierarchy of these tasks, and the results of the tests depended upon how far up the ladder of tasks any particular child could go. The great value of the Binet tests was that they seemed to work, the "normal" children could be separated from the "dull" children.

Basically the construction of intelligence tests has not changed, though a great deal of time and energy has been spent in refining and sharpening the tests. The first major addition to Binet's work in America was made by Lewis Terman, a member of the faculty of Stanford University in California. The result was a test called Stanford-Binet, the oldest and still one of the most widely used American intelligence tests.

Terman tried his tests out on one thousand California students he believed to be representative of the general population. The original Binet tests were translated and items switched from age group to age group, or sometimes dropped entirely, and new ones added. Terman's most significant addition was a vocabulary test. Along with his associates Terman compiled a list of words by selecting the last word in every sixth column in a standard dictionary. These words were arranged in order of difficulty. The testers postulated that each word on the list represented approximately one hundred and fifty words of the student's vocabulary. A person who knew 50 of the words on the list would, by this calculation, have a working vocabulary of about 7,500 words. The vocabulary test was, in Terman's view, the single most important part of his test.

What is an I.Q. test like? For young children the individually administered Stanford-Binet I.Q. tests involve a lot of props—cards with pictures, toys, and other objects—because young children can't read or write. But even in these tests the success or failure of the child depends heavily upon how many words he knows. A two-year-old is asked to name parts of the body on a paper doll. Another task is to identify pictures of common objects. Two-year-olds ought to be able to name three out of eighteen of these.

As the age level of the tests increase, more and more verbal items are added. Five-year-olds are asked to define common words, while thirteen-year-olds are supposed to rearrange a scrambled sentence. After the age of six a vocabulary list is part of the procedure for everyone.

The entire Stanford-Binet I.Q. test may take anywhere from half an hour for young children to nearly an hour for adults. The reason is that adults' answers may range over a wide span of mental levels, and it takes some time before their "mental age" can be established.

Evelyn Sharp, a writer on education and a severe critic of I.Q. testing, contends in her book *The IQ Cult* that the entire concept of "mental age" is outmoded. "For one thing, it tends to give the impression that two children with the same mental age have the same kind of mind. This is not true. If a seven-year-old and a twelve-year-old each have a mental age of ten, they both get the same number of items right, but probably not the same items. They arrived at their scores by different paths. In all likelihood, the bright younger child earned his credits on tasks requiring analysis and judgment, the dull older child on tasks based on factual information that comes from schooling or experience."

Next to the Stanford-Binet series the most popular intelligence tests are the Wechsler tests or Wechsler Intelligence Scale (WIS). These were first developed by David Wechsler, a clinical psychologist at Bellevue Hospital in New York City. They were originally designed for use with adults and later expanded to test children. The test for children is called the Wechsler Intelligence Scale for Children (WISC).

The Wechsler tests abandon the entire concept of mental age. They are not divided by age levels, but rather into ten subtests. A subject can get individual I.Q. scores on each of the subtests, as well as a total I.Q. score for the entire test. The Wechsler test relies less on verbal skills than does the Stanford-Binet.

But despite the differences, if a child takes the Stanford-Binet on one day and the Wechsler on another, he is likely to come out with a similar I.Q. score from both tests. Studies made in the 1960s show a .80 correlation between scores made on the two tests. (A perfect correlation is 1.00.) Close correlation between the scores on different kinds of intelligence tests, as we shall see shortly, is considered extremely important by those who construct the tests.

While many people have never taken an individualized intelligence test, hardly anyone who has grown up and gone to school in America since World War I has escaped taking at least one and more often half a dozen different kinds of group intelligence tests. The most widely used of these are the Otis-Lennon series, based originally on the work of Arthur Otis who developed the basic form for the Army Alpha test.

The group tests do not make the same claims to measuring that elusive quality of innate intelligence as do the individually administered tests. The scores of group tests are not always reported as I.Q.s. On the Otis-Lennon, the subject can be given a percentile score. That shows how he ranked as compared to a group of children his own age whose test scores were used as a standardized sample. A person who scores in the fiftieth percentile is just exactly in the middle of the standardization sample—half the sample group got better scores, half worse.

There are two major and generally acknowledged shortcomings to group tests. The tests are supposed to be given to everyone under exactly the same conditions. In practice this is, of course, impossible. All those who administer the tests read the same booklet explaining how the test is to be conducted, and minor variations in procedure probably don't have much effect on an individual's score. But a teacher who mumbles directions, or who explains more than he is supposed to, or a noisy test room might seriously affect the score of an entire group.

A second problem arises from the fact that most group tests are scored either by machine or hand-graded by using a stencil that shows the correct answers. In such tests the questions must, of necessity, be multiple choice. Answers are indicated by blackening a square. A test subject who is tense or careless or inattentive to directions might score far lower than he or she should. On the other hand, a relaxed and test-wise subject can do quite well simply by guessing. Guessing represents a tricky problem for test makers, and instruction manuals don't have much to say about it. Some tests give demerits for wrong answers, to discourage guessing. In other tests wrong answers have the same value as unanswered questions. The reasons for the difference may have as much to do with the way the tests are scored as with any philosophy about testing or intelligence. In the stencil-scored tests only correct answers show up, whereas in many machine-graded tests wrong answers can be located.

In most cases, however, prudent guessing will help raise a score. If you can eliminate two or three of the five possible choices as obviously wrong, and then take a guess between the remainder as to which is the most likely answer, you will probably gain more than you stand to lose. A drawback is that guessing at questions generally takes longer, so that you may not get as far along on the test as you otherwise would and miss some easy answers later on. All group tests have a strict time limit. A test-wise individual will mark down all the answers he is sure of first, then go back and guess at as many more questions as time will allow.

It seems that simply knowing how to take tests will improve a score. Evelyn Sharp cites an example where a young Mississippi black student raised his I.Q. score dramatically in six weeks simply by being taught how to take tests. Had the young man become more intelligent or just more experienced?

I.Q. tests are also criticized for depending too heavily upon verbal ability—knowing and using words. No one contends that verbal ability is all that there is to intelligence, yet the individual who speaks English poorly is at an extreme and unfair disadvantage in taking any kind of I.Q. test. He may not even be able to properly understand the directions for the test, much less the questions. Attempts to avoid this bias are the so-called culture-free or culture-fair tests. Instead of using vocabulary and definition questions, these tests concentrate on

Data Sufficiency Questions

Directions: Each of the data sufficiency problems below consists of a question and two statements, labeled (1) and (2), in which certain data are given. You have to decide whether the data given in your statements are *sufficient* for answering the question. Using the data given in the statements *plus* your knowledge of mathematics and everyday facts (such as the number of days in July or the meaning of *counterclockwise*), you are to black space.

A if statement (1) ALONE is sufficient, but statement (2) alone is not sufficient to answer the question asked;

B if statement (2) ALONE is sufficient, but statement (1) alone is not sufficient to answer the question asked;

C if BOTH statements (1) and (2) TOGETHER are sufficient to answer the question asked, but NEITHER statement ALONE is sufficient;

D if EACH statement ALONE is sufficient to answer the question asked;

E if statements (1) and (2) TOGETHER are NOT sufficient to answer the question asked, and additional data specific to the problem are needed.

In a four-volume work, what is the weight of the third volume?
(1) The four-volume work weighs 8 pounds.
(2) The first three volumes together weigh 6 pounds.

A portion of the Otis-Lennon Mental Ability Test.

testing the recognition of relationships among different types of figures and designs. These tests are the descendants of the Army Beta tests.

In theory the culture-free tests could be given to a college professor's son, a ghetto-raised child of a welfare family, and a child in a family of Cambodian peasants, and all the scores would be meaningfully comparable. Some initial evidence indicates that people from various cultures do get the same range of scores on culture-free tests. But the solid proof that such tests are significant is still lacking.

Another test many are likely to encounter is the Scholastic Aptitude Test, or SAT. This test can be taken anywhere in the world. The purpose of the SAT is to predict how well students will do academically. In fact, this warning is issued with the test: "Any claims that aptitude tests now in use really measure intelligence or general mental ability may or may not be substantiated."

In practice, however, most people who give such tests or take them do seem to regard them as proven measures of intelligence. In achieving the limited purpose for which they were designed, that is, predicting how well a student will do in school, the SAT has been quite effective. Actually though, it is almost as easy to predict a student's future grades by looking at his present grades and ignoring aptitude tests entirely. The confusion between school success and intelligence is both deep and widespread. When this confusion is reinforced by aptitude test scores, then most people assume the students with the highest grades are innately the most intelligent.

How can we be sure that intelligence tests test anything significant? For example, if a majority of ten-year-olds could identify the winner of last year's World Series, would this provide us with any information about the basic intelligence of the group? In the view of those who construct tests, there are two ways to check test validity.

Sample SAT Questions

I. VERBAL QUESTIONS
Analogies

Directions: In the following question, a related pair of words is followed by five lettered pairs of words. Select the lettered pair which best expresses a relationship *similar* to that expressed in the original pair.

CISTERN: WATER: (A) shower: cloud (B) official: power (C) science: matter (D) museum: antiques (E) vault: valuables

Antonyms (*Opposites*)

Directions: The question below consists of a word printed in capital letters, followed by five words lettered A through E. Choose the lettered word which is most nearly *opposite* in meaning to the word in capital letters.

COMPOSURE: (A) analysis (B) alertness (C) contrast (D) agitation (E) destruction

Sentence Completions

Directions: The sentence below has a blank space, indicating that a word has been omitted. Beneath the sentence are five lettered words. You are to choose the one word which, when inserted in the sentence, *best* fits in with the meaning of the sentence as a whole.

High yields of food crops per acre accelerate the —— of soil nutrients.
(A) depletion (B) erosion (C) cultivation (D) fertilization (E) conservation

II. MATHEMATICAL QUESTIONS
Standard Multiple-Choice Questions

Directions: Indicate the *one* correct answer in the appropriate space on the answer sheet.

If $16 \times 16 \times 16 = 8 \times 8 \times P$, the $P =$
(A) 4 (B) 8 (C) 32 (D) 48 (E) 64

The first is, of course, that the people who score well on the tests also generally do better in school than those who score less well. This would not necessarily be the case with those who could answer questions about baseball.

The problem here is that there are a large number of possible reasons why a person might do well in school and also score well on I.Q. tests. The ability to sit still and follow directions would help in both test-taking and school, but would this be a sign of intelligence? Conversely there may be a large number of reasons why an individual would do poorly on an intelligence test and in school, and still be quite intelligent. Yet test makers believe that the correlation between school success and high test scores is a strong indicator of the value of their tests.

A second way of checking out the value of intelligence tests is their internal consistency. Those who construct the tests assume that they are probing some kind of innate ability. This ability should logically be distributed through the population in a "normal" way. When the test results from a representative sample of the population are charted on a graph they should fall into the familiar bell-shaped curve. The closer the test results conform to the "normal" distribution, the better they are thought to be.

One assumption we work with is that I.Q. is a relatively fixed quantity. The test makers have expended a great deal of energy constructing tests that will yield consistent scores year after year. If a child gets an I.Q. score of 105 at the age of five, his score should remain at about that level for the rest of his life. Most test scores do work out that way.

In making up an intelligence test, questions probing a variety of different abilities are included. There are questions concerning verbal abilities, spatial relations, ability to handle numbers, and so forth. Do people who do well in one of these areas generally do well in others?

This really depends primarily on the philosophy of those who made up the test in the first place. The philosophy behind the most widely used intelligence tests holds that while there are many different aspects to intelligence, all the parts are intimately related. Therefore, in making up the tests, questions are chosen that involve different areas of ability, but in practice can be answered correctly by most people at any given level.

On some other tests, in which the philosophy of the test makers is that there is a wide difference between these basic abilities, very different results may be produced. The average test subject may do quite well on some parts of these tests, but quite poorly on others.

A further method of checking the validity of I.Q. tests is to compare the scores received on one type of test against those received on a slightly different type of test. If the scores tend to match, it is often assumed that both tests are working properly. Most of the popular tests do match quite closely, though not perfectly. The Mensa organization had trouble with its tests because the variation it allowed was quite narrow.

Huge volumes have been written, filled with columns of statistics concerning the "validation" of intelligence tests. Millions of tests have been given, and scores tabulated and compared in endless computer print-outs. This data has a satisfying feel of solidity about it, at least for those who give the tests. To the general public this mass of validation may give the impression that the I.Q. score is something as tangible and real as a measurement of height or weight. Proponents of I.Q. testing often behave as if this were the case.

But there really is no such solidity to I.Q. data. The whole structure by which I.Q. tests are validated is quite artificial. Many of the statistical methods used by behavioral scientists were first developed for use in the physical sciences. Though perhaps reasonable to the nonstatistician, physical scientists are often unimpressed, and sometimes downright angry, over the way behavioral scientists, and I.Q. testers in particular, present their theories as proven facts. David Layzer, an astronomer from Harvard, has criticized the basic assumptions upon which the whole theory of I.Q. scores as a measure of intelligence depends in an article in the book *The Fallacy of I.Q.* The assumption that there is a single underlying ability called intelligence is dismissed as "pure metaphysics. Assertions about the existence of unobservable properties cannot be proved or disproved; their acceptance demands an act of faith."

Doesn't the "normal" distribution of I.Q. scores among the population prove that the quantity the test measures is some innate aspect of people? Not necessarily, says Layzer, because there really is no such thing as "normal" distribution. He quotes the great French mathematician Jules Henri Poincaré: "Everybody believes in it [normal distribution]: the experimenters because they think it has been proved by mathematics, the mathematicians because it has been established by observation." Layzer continues: "Nowadays, both experimenters and mathematicians know better."

Some types of measurements of human accomplishment simply do not fall into the pleasing bell-shaped curve of "normal" distribution. "Golf scores," says Layzer, "are not likely to be normally distributed."

Considering that we do not really know what intelligence is, there is nothing at all improper about constructing tests as modern intelligence tests have been constructed. In the end it may turn out that those who have criticized the tests have been too harsh, or altogether wrong. We just do not know, and most people do not understand just how theoretical and uncertain the whole intelligence testing business still is.

In *Human Intelligence: Its Nature and Assessment,*

one of the most comprehensive accounts of intelligence testing currently available, H. J. Butcher, professor of higher education at the University of Manchester, England, remarks, somewhat ironically: ". . . in practice, the constructors with the confidence of practitioners in a well charted area, are generally content with specific criteria, such as correlation with a well established test or adequate prediction of scholastic achievement."

An even stronger criticism has been made by the British psychologist Joanna Ryan in a chapter written for the book *Race and Intelligence*. "This attitude to validation is the source of much mystification about what I.Q. scores mean, mystification which is unfortunately increased by the internal techniques of quantification that give intelligence tests a largely spurious appearance of scientific respectability."

Those who make up the tests are perhaps naturally impressed by the way that they are able to make their tests conform so neatly to statistical models. But Joanna Ryan complains that: "the technique of test construction has become an end in itself . . . this preoccupation with the techniques of measurement has meant that relatively little attention has been paid to the substantial content of tests, and to their validity as tests of intelligence."

Unfortunately the public at large has only a vague and largely incorrect notion of how intelligence tests work. The complicated pro and con arguments concerning various aspects of testing are rarely heard, and people go on assuming that somehow "science" has set up a solid scale, like a thermometer or a ruler, that measures intelligence, and that I.Q. scores show where an individual ranks on that scale.

The many different kinds of intelligence tests create a problem, for each operates in a somewhat different way, and each is supposed to give a truer measure of intelligence than the others. Yet Prof. Butcher, a man who believes in the value of intelligence testing, rather than a critic of the practice, has pointed out the wide divergence in philosophies about tests among the leading psychologists:

"The study of high-level human abilities is fundamentally much less advanced in spite of the mass of published research, and the degree of divergence among authoritative experts will rapidly become apparent. If Gulford believes that some 120 independent measurable abilities are required to describe human capacity, whereas Vernon finds that general intelligence accounts for far more variation than all the other factors put together in representative samples, whether of children or adults; and if Cattell asserts that with a 'culture-fair' test he can derive scores that are genuinely comparable, obtained from Americans, Italians and Formosans, whereas educational sociologists question the significance of differences in measured ability within a single school in one country, we are still a long way from establishing the agreement on valid procedure that is one important sign of a developed science."

Despite all controversy, however, general correlation between scores of major intelligence tests remains. It is fair to assume that intelligence tests do measure *something*. Whether this something is a general factor we can call intelligence is a question that simply cannot be answered at this time.

Besides the fact that the results of the tests can be made to conform to a statistical model, do they do anything else? Is the *something* the tests measure a significant quantity in any way?

I.Q. tests have been seen to be pretty good predictors of how well a student will do in school, and how long he or she will stay in school. But one can hardly be surprised since from the very beginning the tests were validated by school success. That is, tests which seemed to pick out good students were considered good tests, and those that did not were dropped. But are I.Q. tests useful for predicting anything else—for example success in later life?

The answer to that question is apparently not. Christopher Jencks of Harvard and a group of his associates surveyed most of the available information about intelligence testing, education, and social and economic status in America. The results were published in *Inequality: A Reassessment of the Effect of Family and Schooling in America.* Jencks's unexpected conclusion was: "Scores on the tests show remarkably little relation to performance in most adult roles. People with high scores do a little better in most jobs than people with low scores, and they earn somewhat more money, but the differences are surprisingly small."

Surprising indeed, for intelligence, or in the very least scholastic achievement, would seem to be a very good thing to possess in making one's way in the modern world. But in his study of schooling, I.Q., and achievement Jencks came to a very different conclusion. Summarizing his findings in an article in the *Atlantic Monthly,* Jencks and coworker Mary Jo Bane observe: "The fact is that people who do well on I.Q. and achievement tests do not perform much better than the average in most jobs. Nor do they earn much more than the average. There have been more than a hundred studies of the relationship between I.Q. and people's performance on different jobs, using a wide variety of techniques for rating performance. In general, differences in I.Q. account for less than 10 percent of the variation in actual job performance. In many situations, there is no relationship at all between a man's I.Q. and how competent he is at his job. I.Q. also plays a modest role in determining income, explaining only about 12 percent of the variation. Thus, 88 percent of the variation in income is unrelated to I.Q."

Why, then, do some people succeed and others fail? Jencks and his associates can offer no easy answers to such a question. The social and economic background of an individual seems to count about as much as his I.Q. score. Beyond that, a wide variety of skills exist that have no relationship to I.Q. "The ability to hit a ball thrown at high speed is extremely valuable, if you happen to be a professional baseball player," Jencks notes.

The ability to understand what your boss wants, or to get your subordinates to understand what you want, is an ability that can be at a great premium in a large organization, yet it is not necessarily related to I.Q. Other personal traits, like the ability to inspire trust and confidence, and just plain being likable, are also assets in employment and personal life, that have little or nothing to do with I.Q.

Then there is luck. "America," says Jencks, "is full of gamblers, some of whom strike it rich while others lose hard-earned assets. One man's farm has oil on it, while another man's cattle get hoof-and-mouth disease."

There is an old American saying: "If you're so smart why ain't you rich?" The answer seems to be that "smartness," at least as measured by I.Q. tests, has very little to do with getting rich.

Arthur Jensen

7

Heredity,
Race, and I.Q.

The most emotionally charged question in psychology, indeed, in any branch of science today, comes in two parts: "Is intelligence hereditary, and if so, are there hereditary differences in intelligence among the races?"

The question is not a new one. Sir Francis Galton, with whom the study of human intelligence really began, believed very strongly that intelligence was mainly hereditary. He was also convinced that there were profound differences in mental ability between the races. He regarded Negroes as barely human at all. "The mistakes the Negroes made in their own matters," he wrote in *Hereditary Genius*, "were so childishly stupid and simpleton-like as frequently made me ashamed of my own species." Such views were not at all unusual for a Victorian Englishman who had spent some years in Africa.

Galton's opinions and those of his contemporaries were based on subjective impressions and prejudice. There could be no definitive statements about innate mental differences because at the end of the nineteenth century there had been no effective intelligence testing.

The first mass intelligence testing program, the Army tests given upon America's entry into World War I, seemed to indicate some racial factors. Whites generally did better than blacks, but the results were not necessarily signs of hereditary differences. The score any individual got on the Army test was, as we now know, strongly influenced by the amount of education he had received. So blacks from some northern states scored better than whites from some southern states. Such results were very unsettling to white southerners and some asked that the information be suppressed.

While the Army tests seemed to suggest a strong environmental influence on test scores, the Army tests were not pure I.Q. tests and the hereditary theory of intelligence certainly did not disappear.

Pioneer American intelligence tester Lewis Terman was a firm believer in the hereditary basis of I.Q. scores. Over the years Terman and his associates compiled a massive multivolume study of the lives of individuals with high I.Q.s. This work is called *Genetic Studies of Genius*, a title clearly reminiscent of Galton's *Hereditary Genius*. The basic conclusion of the Terman study was that smart people have smart children, and dull people have dull children.

In 1925 Terman issued a blunt challenge to his critics who believed that environment largely determined I.Q. scores:

"There are . . . many persons who believe that intelligence quotients can be manufactured to order by the application of suitable methods of training. There are even prominent educators and psychologists who are inclined to regard such a pedagogical feat as within the realm of possibility, and no one knows that it is not. It is possible it is time we were finding out. Conclusive evidence as to the extent to which I.Q.s can be artificially raised could be supplied in a few years by an experiment which would cost a few hundred thousand or at most a few million dollars. The knowledge would probably be worth to humanity a thousand times that amount."

Terman's theories about the hereditary nature of intelligence were not popular among social scientists during the 1930s. The politically liberal environmental school of social science held that most of the differences in I.Q. scores were due to outside influences, primarily the nature of an individual's upbringing and schooling. Still, few even among the environmentalists doubted that there was a significant, though entirely unknown, hereditary component to intelligence.

Most elementary texts on psychology contained the story of the Jukes and Kalikaks, two families that had been traced over six generations, and had produced a depressingly large number of criminals and mental defectives. These families were contrasted with the Adams family which had had two Presidents and a host of other distinguished men and women in its genealogy.

Nor could anyone deny the existence of major genetic differences between the races. Skin color, which is genetically determined, is only the most obvious of these differences. There are many other hereditary physical differences. But whether there might also be hereditary mental differences among the races was a problem that most social scientists preferred to avoid, either because too little was known about mental processes, or because the subject was considered too hot to handle.

Thus the environmentalists, while not denying the influence of heredity on intelligence, were not very concerned with it either. Heredity could not be altered, and the environmentalists concentrated on what they thought could be improved.

During and after World War II all theories that implied hereditary mental differences among races were suspected of being tainted with fascism. Hitler and the Nazis had used spurious theories of racial inferiority to justify their genocide. Psychologists and educators recoiled from any sort of racial theories with real horror.

Yet despite American hatred and denunciation of Nazi racial theories, segregation of the races had remained a way of life for most Americans. In the south segregation was legally sanctioned. In much of the north segregation, though informal, was nonetheless rigid.

But for the first time since the Civil War American traditions of racial segregation came under serious and sustained attack. In 1954 the United States Supreme Court struck down the principle of segregated schools. These schools were supposed to be "separate but equal." In practice the white schools were a lot more "equal" in every respect than the black ones.

The 1954 court decision marked the beginning of the end for the more visible forms of segregation in both the south and the north. The goal of a thoroughly integrated educational system is, however, still far from being a reality, as the seemingly unending series of court cases, administrative decisions, and boycotts and other disruptions indicates. Still there can be little serious argument with the observation that a black child has a better chance of getting a good education in the 1970s than he had during the 1920s.

The 1960s was the decade of civil rights. The federal government, motivated partly out of genuine concern for blacks and other minority groups, and partly under intense pressure from militant groups that were literally bursting the bounds of the ghetto, moved to try to make up for past inequalities. The most ambitious action was taken in the area of education. Education seemed the best hope for improving the position of the disadvantaged segments of American society.

A large number of programs, like Head Start for preschoolers, were begun. These programs were supported by substantial grants of money from the Federal government. They were aimed at helping poor youngsters, white as well as black, get the same sort of educational opportunities as children born into the white middle class.

Despite ambitious starts and a few notable successes, by 1969 there was a general feeling of disappointment and disillusionment with most of these programs. The minority groups had failed to catch up academically and the programs had not led to any widespread improvement in minority I.Q. scores.

What had gone wrong? In the winter of 1969 Professor Arthur Jensen of the University of California, one of the nation's leading educational psychologists, suggested an explosive answer to this question. The most forceful expression of Jensen's view appeared in an article he wrote for the *Harvard Educational Review*, a magazine normally unknown to those outside of the educational field. Yet within a few weeks quotations from this technical article in an obscure publication had been picked up by *Time, Newsweek, U.S. News and World Report, The New York Times,* and at least a dozen syndicated columnists. It had even been discussed at a meeting of President Nixon's cabinet.

Jensen, a mild-mannered and relatively unknown scholar in a usually quiet field, had suddenly become one of the most famous and notorious people in the country. He was denounced by many as a racist, and a flood of hate mail and crank calls came into his home and office. Radical students broke up his class and he was forced to give his lectures at a secret location. For a time he even feared for his life. On the other side, he suddenly became the darling of segregationists who took to citing his article in court as the final word of "science" and proof that integration would not work.

The title of Jensen's shattering article was a deceptively bland question: "How Much Can We Boost I.Q. and Scholastic Achievement?" Jensen's answer was a qualified but definite "not much." Why not? According to Jensen, I.Q. and thus scholastic achievement depend largely upon heredity, and therefore no amount of special education is going to equalize basic inborn inequalities. What made Jensen's article especially volatile was that he stressed the racial element in the distribution of I.Q. scores. He made a point of reminding his readers that over the years blacks have averaged about 15 points lower on I.Q. tests than whites or Orientals.

The general view among liberal educators was that the racial differences were due largely to the social and economic disadvantages suffered by blacks, and that compensatory education could close the gap. Jensen's conclusion was quite different. He began his article: "Compensatory education has been tried and it apparently has failed.

"Compensatory education has been practiced on a massive scale for several years in many cities across the nation. It began with auspicious enthusiasm and high hopes of educators. It had unprecedented support from Federal funds. It has theoretical sanction from social scientists espousing the major underpinning of its rationale: the 'deprivation hypothesis,' according to which academic lag is mainly the result of social, economic, and educational deprivation and discrimination—an hypothesis that has met with wide, uncritical acceptance in the atmosphere of society's growing concern about the plight of minority groups and the economically disadvantaged.

"The chief goal of compensatory education—to remedy the educational lag of disadvantaged children and thereby narrow the achievement gap between 'minority' and 'majority' pupils—has been utterly unrealized in any of the large compensatory education programs that have been evaluated so far."

According to Jensen Lewis Terman's challenge, issued forty-four years earlier, to see if training could improve I.Q. scores had been attempted and had failed. I.Q., Jensen said, was mainly determined by heredity.

If Jensen's theories on the hereditary nature of intelligence were correct the consequences could be profound, and affect far more than the relative positions of blacks and whites in America. Some believe that the hereditary I.Q.s might ultimately determine the structure of American society as a whole.

In the book *Inequality* Jencks and his associates concluded that I.Q. had a relatively minor effect upon what sort of a job an individual got, or how well he did on the job. I.Q., they said, was only one of many factors, and far from the most important one. However, not all social scientists have agreed with this conclusion. In the wake of the Jensen controversy over heredity and I.Q. a lot of older studies that appear to link I.Q. and employment, have been revived and reexamined.

For example, some studies have shown that people with high-status jobs generally have higher I.Q.s than those with low-status jobs. In 1945 T. W. Harrell and M. S. Harrell examined the I.Q.s of a large sample of enlisted men in the Air Force. The men were drawn from seventy-four civilian occupations. In the group, accountants ranked highest, having an average I.Q. of 128.1. Teamsters were the lowest, with an average I.Q. of 87.7.

This finding has been supported by other studies in other countries. For example, in 1961 the British psychologist Sir Cyril Burt studied people in a borough of London. He divided them into six groups on the basis of occupation and social class. In the highest socio-economic group the average I.Q. score was 139.7, whereas in the lowest it was 84.9, a staggering difference of nearly 55 I.Q. points.

This raw I.Q. data must be handled cautiously, and is open to a wide variety of interpretations. But let us assume, as some social scientists do, that I.Q. is both important and hereditary, and we arrive at some very unsettling conclusions about where modern Western society is going. On the surface it might seem that high I.Q. people get better jobs and that, in our open society, smarter people move up in class while duller people move down. But social scientists also know that people have a strong tendency to marry within their own social class. The result would be that high I.Q. people marry one another and have high I.Q. children. The same is true at the other end of the I.Q. scale. Usually people with either very high or very low I.Q.s tend to have children whose I.Q.s are closer to the average. This is what geneticists call the "regression toward the mean."

But despite this tendency, in a few generations the high I.Q. people would become the rich and powerful, and the less intelligent people would become a permanent under-class with little or no chance of rising from their positions of poverty and powerlessness. The ancient ideas of aristocracy, which were supposed to have been swept out of American society at the time of the nation's founding, would be reestablished on a firmer basis than ever before.

Why hasn't this already happened? According to social theorists who envision a caste system based upon intelligence, it is because the open society is a relatively new development. Despite oft repeated success stories, it was rare for the poor farm boy, no matter how intelligent, to rise from poverty to wealth by his own efforts. A century ago rigid barriers of social discrimination kept even very bright students from attending the "best" schools, and as a result, they were generally kept out of the best jobs as well. Without the graduated income tax, wealth was more easily passed from generation to generation, no matter how unworthy the heir might be. But some believe that the old barriers of social class have broken down, and that the more intelligent will inevitably rise to the top of the social scale.

Writing in the September 1971 issue of the *Atlantic Monthly* magazine, Harvard psychologist Richard Herrenstein foresaw a rigidly stratified society, based on a caste of intelligence:

"Greater wealth, health, freedom, fairness and educational opportunity are not going to give us the egalitarian society of our philosophical heritage. It will instead give us a society sharply graduated, with ever greater innate separation between the top and the bottom, and ever more uniformity within families as far as inherited abilities are concerned. . . . The vista reminds us of the world we had hoped to leave behind—aristocracies, privileged classes, unfair advantages and disadvantages of birth. But it is different for the privileged classes of the past were probably not much superior biologically to the downtrodden, which is why revolutions had a fair chance of success. By removing aribitrary barriers between the classes, society has encouraged the creation of biological barriers. When people can freely take their natural level in society, the upper classes will, virtually by definition, have greater capacity than the lower."

Herrenstein's vision is of a sort of Brave New World with sharply divided classes based on biologically determined mental abilities. "The biological stratification of society would surely go on whether we had tests to gauge it or not, but with them a more humane and tolerant grasp of human differences is possible." He concludes rather wanly: "and at the moment, that seems our best hope." Herrenstein based his predictions mainly on Jensen's theories.

In England Professor H. J. Eysinck advanced the idea of hereditary intelligence in his book *I.Q. Argument, Race, Intelligence and Education.* Actually the idea had always been more popular in Britain than in the United States. Jensen had studied with Eysinck in England. Still,

Eysinck's theories struck a newly tender spot in an England which was then beginning to experience the same racial conflicts that have plagued America for many generations.

Neither Jensen nor Eysinck presented any new ideas or evidence. Similar ideas had often been put forth in the past, and had gone virtually unnoticed. Yet in the years since Jensen's article was first published, the furor has, if anything, increased. Whether we like it or not, Jensenism, as the theory of hereditary racial differences in I.Q. has come to be called, must be faced.

Jensen's argument rests on a few basic points. The first is that I.Q. measures something important. Jensen himself was quite careful and circumspect in defining intelligence. He called it the "particular constellation of abilities we call 'intelligence' and which we can measure by means of 'intelligence tests.' " This I.Q. factor, he was quick to emphasize, was only part of the range of human ability but one that "has been singled out from the total galaxy of mental abilities as being especially important in our society mainly because of the nature of our traditional system of formal education and occupation structure with which it is coordinated." Jensen also said that "as far as we know the full range of human talents is represented in all the major races of man."

In a previous chapter we looked at some of the difficulties surrounding the I.Q. test and what it is supposed to measure. Because of Jensen's influence, blacks and others who feel that they are being oppressed by I.Q. tests have intensified their attack on the use of the tests. But since the majority of the population still consider I.Q. a measure of something important, we cannot just dismiss the points raised by Jensen because there is no general agreement about the value of the tests themselves. Let us simply assume for the moment that whatever I.Q. is, it is something worth consideration.

Jensen believes that the best evidence for the heritability of I.Q. comes from studies of identical twins done some years ago in England by Sir Cyril Burt and geneticist J. A. Shields. Identical twins are excellent subjects for genetic studies since genetically they are the same.

The British scientists examined one hundred pairs of identical twins who had been split up and raised in different homes. They found that among the separated twins the difference in I.Q. was only 6 points. By contrast, any two people chosen at random from the population will have an average I.Q. difference of 18 points. To Jensen this study seemed to indicate that common genes account for 75 to 80 percent of an I.Q. score. Even when raised in different environments, genetically identical individuals had very nearly the same I.Q. scores.

In contrast to the finding about twins, unrelated children reared in the same home often have very different I.Q.s. "If you look at the studies of adopted children," says Jensen, "you find that their intelligence relates more closely to their natural parents than to their adoptive parents." The average difference in I.Q.s between a randomly selected pair is about 18 points whereas among adopted children who have shared the same home environment after the age of six months, the average difference in I.Q. scores is about 15 points.

Still the bulk of the evidence has always suggested that there is some genetic factor in I.Q. The problem has always been, how big a factor is it? Jensen's estimate of 80 percent is an educated guess and a high one. Other investigators such as Christopher Jencks have arrived tentatively at a figure around 50 percent, while others suggest a lower figure still. All of these figures can only be educated guesses, nothing more.

However, there are some serious objections to basing theories on studies of this type. The twins studies cover only a small number of children, not Americans, nor are the studies very recent. In the studies of adopted children different investigators measured I.Q. in different ways, and the range of environmental variation was very great. As a result, different investigators came to different conclusions about what they found. In short, this evidence for the heritability of I.Q. is far from unambiguous.

Furthermore the studies of twins and adopted children were confined to whites. To apply these findings as a measure of difference between blacks and whites would be very uncertain. In general, blacks in America are poorer, receive less education, and have lower-status jobs than do whites. However, Jensen says: "When you control samples of white and black populations for social class differences you still have major differences in I.Q. between them from 15 points on the average to 11 points over the various social classes."

But are such differences due only to heredity? The evidence is not as clear as it first appears. The fact that a black and a white child both have fathers who do the same kind of work or mothers who spent the same number of years in school does not mean the two children are treated the same way, either at home or elsewhere. Jewish children also do better on I.Q. tests than Christian children of the same socio-economic level, but very few people conclude that Jews are genetically superior to Christians. Instead we conclude that Jews treat their children differently from Christians even when their occupations, incomes, and education are the same.

Some of the factors which may enter in here are prenatal and postnatal care, patterns of child rearing, the early effects of discrimination and low expectations, even nutrition. Since we do not know what I.Q. is, it is quite impossible to say with any confidence what will affect it.

Another problem frequently pointed out by Jensen's critics is that I.Q. tests have been standardized almost totally with white, middle-class Americans. Proponents of

I.Q. testing counter that other groups of nonwhites—American Indians for example—who are severely disadvantaged economically do quite well on I.Q. tests. But the data here is much less complete and persuasive.

The mechanics of heritability present a further complication. Patterns of inheritance among white Americans have been studied rather thoroughly, but we know a great deal less about patterns of heritability among American blacks. Are they the same as among whites, or do the patterns of inheritance differ greatly? We simply don't know, and a difference might have a considerable effect upon the distribution of I.Q. scores.

Jensen's conclusion that I.Q.s cannot be raised significantly has also been sharply attacked. His statement that compensatory education has been tried and failed may well be premature and too harsh. True enough, educational programs like Head Start did not result in significant jumps in the I.Q.s of students enrolled in them. But does this mean that I.Q.s cannot be raised, or does it simply mean that the programs so far have been using the wrong techniques?

Besides, not all the programs have failed. In Milwaukee, Wisconsin, a special project involving the infants of extremely poor and low I.Q. mothers has produced dramatic results according to Stephen Strickland, former director of the National Advisory Council on the Education of Disadvantaged Children. Practically from birth these children were given intensive attention by a group of social workers, teachers, and doctors. The mothers too were often given training in homemaking and baby care. At forty-three months of age the children in the active stimulation group measured an average of 33 I.Q. points higher than children in the control group. These children in the experimental program also seemed to learn at a rate generally in excess of the norm for their age peers.

One really can't jump to any conclusions from this

single project. In the first place only a small number of individuals is involved—about forty children in all—and although the project has been going on for some years the results cannot yet be evaluated completely. In addition it deals specifically with extremely low I.Q. families. It is possible that special attention will improve the I.Q. scores of very deprived children, but will do little for children whose home environments are more within a more normal range.

There is, however, more evidence for the improvement of I.Q.s. In Israel, the I.Q.s of Oriental Jews from backward countries have been increased significantly when they are placed in communes called kibbutzim and brought up collectively rather than by their biological parents.

Taken together these findings hint that I.Q. scores may rise if a deprived child's environment is changed drastically; perhaps educational programs like Head Start are simply too little and too late.

Another factor which must be weighed in the racial I.Q. controversy is the subtle effect of discrimination. Despite much talk of equality, white Americans have generally considered black Americans innately inferior, and treated them as such. Discrimination was going on a long time before Jensen wrote his article, and a long time before there was any such thing as an I.Q. test. As a result blacks have often come to consider themselves inferior, particularly where I.Q. tests are concerned. When asked to estimate their own I.Q.s blacks usually give estimates far lower in comparison to their actual tests scores than do whites.

Psychologist Irwin Katz thought that merely taking an I.Q. test might be a stressful situation for blacks—and that the effects of stress would lower their scores. He set up an experiment to explore this idea. Katz gave an identical set of questions to two groups of blacks. One set of questions was called a research exercise while the other was labeled an I.Q. test. The blacks did much worse when they thought that they were taking an I.Q. test than when doing a research exercise.

The mere presence of a white tester also seems to create stress. As early as 1936 researchers found that blacks averaged 6 points better on I.Q. tests when tested by other blacks than when tested by whites. All of these studies were collected in *Social Class, Race and Psychological Development*, edited by Martin Deutsch, Katz and ironically perhaps, Arthur Jensen.

British psychologist Peter Watson, who reviewed the evidence on stress, race, and I.Q. tests, concluded: "It would seem therefore, that there is at least a double handicap to your intellectual performance when you are black: 1. the white environment, particularly in America, is threatening and stressful, evoking reactions that are a drain on your performance; 2. your expectancy of success is low (realistically usually) and this only makes matters worse. In testing disadvantaged groups, much less attention has been paid to these handicaps than to those arising from differences in upbringing, or in the case of immigrants from language problems."

Watson fears that the newly popular ideas about the genetic differences in intelligence will produce one of the worst drains on intellectual performance among blacks. The statements about blacks having low I.Q.s will sadly become self-fulfilling prophecies.

Jensen and his supporters have answered, or attempted to answer, all of the criticisms that have been raised by his opponents. The answers have in turn provoked more criticism and more answers and so forth and so forth. Nothing has been resolved, nor is anything likely to be resolved, for the heated and lengthy argument has brought out little that was not known, or at least widely suspected, concerning the distribution of I.Q. scores for the last ten or twenty years.

Before Jensen, a Nobel prize-winning physicist, William Shockley, tried to call attention to possible genetic differences in intelligence among the races. Since Shockley was a physicist and not a psychologist his ideas did not provoke the furor Jensen kicked up. However, Shockley's pronouncements did move the National Academy of Sciences, one of the nation's most prestigious scientific bodies, to declare: "there is no scientific basis for the statement that there are or are not substantial hereditary differences in intelligence between Negro and white populations. In the absence of some unforeseen way of equalizing all aspects of environment, the answers to this question can hardly be more than reasonable guesses."

Jensen considers such an attitude a head-in-the-sand approach to an important question. He asserts that it would be possible to set up experiments that would decrease the heredity-environment uncertainties. He has looked with favor upon a suggestion that disadvantaged black children be placed in a kibbutzlike setting, as was done with the studied Oriental Jews in Israel, to see if their I.Q.s improve. "I believe science is capable of creating techniques to cut through the complexities, if given a chance. Social scientists should be scientists, not ideologists," Jensen told science reporter Lee Edison in an article published in the *New York Times Magazine* of Aug. 31, 1969.

However, we are dealing with human beings, not laboratory animals, and it is not so easy to shift children from one environment to another for the sake of an experiment. Like Galton's genetics, such experiments might be a good idea in theory, but when put into practice the results could be horrifying. Who would have the power to order that children be taken from one environment and placed in another? A society where such experiments could be performed might be one in which none of us would ever care to live.

Jensen believes that the differences in I.Q.s between blacks and whites are more than just a matter of points. He believes that tests indicate blacks are particularly deficient in learning abstract concepts. He suggests that, rather than trying to give everybody an equal education, different students should be placed in different types of programs on the basis of their I.Q. scores. In the *N.Y. Times Magazine* article he was quoted as saying: "Some children will be happiest and most productive learning by rote alone. Others, who have conceptual abilities, should be in classes where they can make the best use of them. If this results in a racial imbalance in classes, so be it. You don't do a service for the child who has a mental age of five if you treat him as though he were seven."

Jensen and like-minded social scientists adopt an attitude that they are merely reporting the scientific facts as they see them. Even though they admit that their case is not conclusive they feel there is no point in hiding from possible facts just because they are unpleasant. Yet there is something unrealistic about this "objectivity." Jensen's theories fit so neatly into an ancient preexisting pattern of prejudice and practice that they could not easily be applied in any "scientific" manner; they would most likely be used to reinforce the prejudices. Rather than stimulating any new research into human or racial differences, these theories are far more likely to serve as props for the status quo. They will also serve as targets of fury for blacks and others who may well feel they are being oppressed by unfair and meaningless I.Q. tests.

Jensen insists that theories about racial differences must not affect the way we treat individuals. "Whenever we select a person for some special educational purpose, whether for special instruction in a grade-school class for children with learning problems, or for a 'gifted' class with an advanced curriculum . . . we are selecting an individual. . . . It is unjust to allow the fact of an individual's racial or social background to affect the treatment accorded to him. All persons rightfully must be regarded on the basis of their individual qualities and merits, and all social, educational and economic institutions must have built into them the mechanisms for insuring and maximizing the treatment of persons according to their individual behavior."

About the only thing that Jensen's supporters and opponents agree upon, is that it is no longer possible to approach the controversy with cool scientific objectivity. A hundred different conclusions can, and have been, drawn from the same body of evidence. The conclusion one arrives at depends as much on emotion as reason.

A really dangerous element of the debate is that it is not being conducted in some sort of academic vacuum—it is being conducted in the real world, where the problems of race and education are pressing in on us every day. The great point spread between black and white I.Q.s is undeniable. The reasons for this spread, indeed the value of the I.Q. test itself, are debatable. We should be humble enough to admit our ignorance about intelligence. But people don't act that way. Jensen's arguments are already being cited as "evidence" that we should abandon our traditional goals of equal education for all.

Jensen's statements that all persons should be regarded on the basis of individual merit rather than racial background, are doubtless sincere and noble, but they are also foolishly unrealistic. Making the idea of racial mental inferiority more scientifically respectable, as Jensen has done, will certainly result in having people treated more like racial stereotypes than individuals.

This is going to remain a genuine scientific controversy for a long time. One is left with the feeling that our society should try to provide the best possible education for all individuals until such a time as we know a good deal more about the subject of intelligence than we do today, and until we have a society where people really can be treated as individuals, and all individuals would be treated humanely. But that is not going to happen. With scientists literally at one another's throats over Jensenism it is not too difficult to imagine what is going to happen —indeed what is already happening—when politicians get hold of theories; when a debased version of Jensenism is injected into a controversy over a local school board; or when white parents inform their child that science has "proven" that blacks are inferior to whites. Like it or not, that is the level at which the race and intelligence controversy is going to be conducted in this country.

Realizing that the problem cannot be resolved or avoided, Christopher Jencks in an article "What Color is I.Q.?—Intelligence and Race"—that appeared in *The New Republic* in 1969 has attempted to put it into some sort of perspective:

"I.Q., whatever its origin, plays a relatively modest role in determining a man's life chances. Even if the I.Q. differences between blacks and whites have a genetic as well as an environmental basis, such differences have very little to do with the way blacks and whites are treated in contemporary America. Otis Dudley Ducan has shown, for example, that blacks with high I.Q.s are almost as disadvantaged economically as those with low I.Q.s. They are also disadvantaged in almost every other respect, from their dealings with the police to their dealings with landlords. Low I.Q.s are not the cause of America's racial problems and higher I.Q.s would not solve these problems. Any white reader who doubts this should simply ask himself whether he would trade the genes which make his skin white for genes which would raise his I.Q. 15 points."

8

Intelligence from the Inside

So far, all our attempts to classify and measure human intelligence have been at best qualified successes, and intelligence testing has been a mixed blessing for our society. We can determine what a person's I.Q. score is, but there is little agreement on what the scores mean, and even less about how individuals with different scores should be treated.

The problem may not so much be that we are not getting the right answers to questions about intelligence, but that we are not asking the right questions in the first place. Instead of trying to find out how intelligent a person is we might be better off trying to find out how a person learns. In most tests of animal intelligence the scientists are not so much trying to measure the creature's intelligence but trying to find out why it reacts as it does.

Alfred Binet, the French psychologist who began intelligence testing around the turn of the century, was really more interested in studying the process of learning than in the rating of intelligence. Rating intelligence was just a practical expedient to Binet, not an end in itself.

Binet noticed that, quite apart from the score that any particular child might make on one of his tests, each child appeared to have a very different way of perceiving and reacting to the world. Even more significantly a child's method of solving a problem was often very different from an adult's, and the method of problem solving, indeed of thinking itself, changed as the child grew. It was wrong, Binet felt, to judge a child's reasoning by adult standards.

Finding out how a child reasons and reacts is a tedious business that requires long hours of close observation. Binet made most of his observations with his own two daughters, Madeleine and Alice. Alice was larger, stronger, and more active and impulsive, and consequently she was much harder to test than Madeleine, who was more serious and less easily distracted.

Not surprisingly, Binet tried more of his tests on Madeleine than on Alice. When Madeleine was a little over a year and a half old Binet showed her a series of outline sketches of familiar objects. The child recognized many of the pictures, such as those of a hat and a chair and an umbrella. But she misidentified pictures of a finger, a mouth, and an ear. Three years later Madeleine's ability to recognize objects had increased greatly, but she still was unable to identify parts of the face like a mouth and a nose. Binet came to the conclusion that she had not yet developed the ability to analyze pictures in parts, and since she had only seen mouths and noses as parts of a whole face she could not recognize them when they were shown to her as isolated objects.

Binet was groping in the dark and tried a lot of other experiments, including a good deal of what we now call free association. He would say a word or phrase and then ask the girls what image was conjured up in their minds. Here he found a clear difference between the reactions of his two daughters. The more impulsive Alice often pictured things that were somewhat different from the word or phrase that she was given. For example, when Binet

said the word "elephant" the girl reported seeing the platform in the zoo where the children climbed on the elephant for a ride—but she did not picture the elephant itself. When he asked what image was conjured up by the
phrase, "a blast of wind carried off the roof of the house,"
Alice "saw" a picture in which the railing, not the roof of
the house was missing. The more methodical Madeleine
rarely made mistakes of this kind. These mistakes, by the
way, were not considered wrong answers, but rather examples of the difference between the two girls' ways of
thinking. Binet believed that with Alice sensory images
came so rapidly that she had little control over them,
whereas with Madeleine, she was able to control her
mental images more carefully.

No grand theories about intelligence or the development of learning can be drawn from these studies. In fact,
Binet's reports of this work remain relatively unknown.
Binet followed the progress of his daughters until they
were teen-agers, but was never able to expand upon his
studies. He died in 1911 at the relatively young age of
fifty-four. His tests for rating intelligence became world-
famous, while his attempts to understand what intelligence is were almost forgotten.

The most important figure in the modern study of
the development of thinking is undoubtedly the Swiss
psychologist Jean Piaget. Piaget's scientific background is
a bit unusual. As a student in Switzerland he did most of
his work with snails and other mollusks, but by the time
he came to Paris to study at the Sorbonne, he had given
up mollusks for child psychology.

Shortly after coming to Paris Piaget began working
in a laboratory attached to a public school. His main task
was to translate and standardize certain English psychological tests for use in French schools, not a very exciting
job. Piaget, however, began to approach the work from a
unique angle. Instead of merely tabulating right and

wrong answers on the tests, he tried to find out how and why a child arrived at an answer, particularly a wrong answer. Wrote Piaget: "I continued for about two years to analyze verbal reasoning of normal children by presenting them with various questions and exposing them to tasks involving simple concrete relations of cause and effect. . . . At last I had found my field of research."

Piaget's research got him an appointment to the J. J. Rousseau Institute in Geneva, Switzerland. He had originally intended to stay just a few years, but he stayed for more than fifty, until his retirement a few years ago at the age of seventy-five. During that period he acquired a worldwide reputation and is regarded as the founder of an entirely new school of child psychology.

Piaget has often described himself as a compulsive worker. In over half a century he has produced a staggering number of papers, books, and research reports. His students have added their own writings to the already huge body of Piagetian doctrine which grows impressively year after year. It would be a hopeless task to try to summarize all the work and theories here, but we can give a picture of the approach that Piaget and his followers take toward the subject of intelligence and how it should be examined.

Like Binet, Piaget did much of his early work with his own children. When his daughter Jacqueline was seven months old, Piaget watched her play with a toy duck. When the duck slipped under the covers and out of sight, the baby seemed to lose interest in it—she did not try to look for it. If she could not see it, apparently it did not exist for her. Piaget put the duck near his daughter's hand and, when she tried to grab for it, he covered it with a sheet. She took back her hand and immediately gave up looking for the toy. It had ceased to exist.

Piaget's conclusion from repeated observations of this type was that for children only a few months of age objects were not yet permanent. The infant's world consists of things which appear and disappear—but lack an independent existence. Just discovering that objects continue to exist even when out of sight marks an important early stage in the development of thinking, says Piaget.

He recorded a further development when he tested his son Laurent at the age of nine months. Laurent was interested in a watch and the psychologist hid it under a cover on one side of the baby. Laurent watched his father, lifted the cover, and grabbed the watch. The next time Piaget hid the watch on the other side, but Laurent continued to look for it in the place where he had successfully found it the first time, though he had clearly seen his father hide it in a different place. A few months later, however, Laurent would always find the object in the place where he had seen it disappear.

Piaget labels the first two years of a child's life as the sensory-motor phase. The infant develops from living in a world of shifting and impermanent objects into a world where objects persist even when out of sight and where effect follows cause.

During the next period of development the child's world becomes more concrete and less self-centered. This period runs from about the age of two to the age of four or five. In these years the child realizes, for example, that the moon does not really follow him down the street, and that a person who stands on another side of an object from where he is standing may have an entirely different view of that object.

Piaget has charted the development of a child's thinking in a number of different areas. He is best known for his work in the development of the concept of numbers. The fundamental thing that a child must learn about numbers is that the basic amount doesn't change just because its appearance has been altered—something must be added to it or taken away from it. This seems ob-

At the University of Montreal, scene of
Piagetian experiments on children's thinking
and doing, 4-year-old Diane Audet takes a
form recognition test.

vious to us but it is not at all obvious to a four-year-old
child.

One of Piaget's most famous and frequently repeated
exercises explores this concept. The child is shown two
identical glasses, each filled with the same amount of colored liquid. The contents of one of the glasses is then
poured into a thinner but taller glass, where the level of
the liquid reaches higher than it did in the original container. When children below the age of about seven or
eight were asked which of the two glasses—the short, fat
one or the tall, thin one—contained more liquid, they
would almost invariably reply that the tall, thin one did.

Their reason was that the level of liquid in the glass was higher. The same children also thought that there was more total liquid when the contents of the original container was poured into three smaller containers. But by the time these children reached the age of eight, they gave the correct answer, pointing out that the quantity had not been changed: "It's only been poured out."

As a check on the liquid experiment, Piaget tried a similar one with beads. The experimenter began putting beads into one vessel, and the child put the same number of beads into a different shaped vessel. Despite the fact that the child and the experimenter counted out exactly the same number of beads, when asked which of the containers held more beads, a four- or five-year-old would point to the one with the highest level of beads. Only later does the concept of a stable number exist in the child's mind, even though he may be able to count very well.

The idea of giving "wrong" or "stupid" answers does not exist in Piagetian testing. The aim of the test is not a score, but an understanding of the thinking process. Piaget reported the following encounter with a girl named Ric, who was five years and eleven months old. He showed her a picture of flowers, most of them poppies, but a few bluebells. "Look at these poppies and these bluebells. If I take all the flowers, or if I take the poppies, which will be the biggest bunch?"

"The bunch of poppies, because there are more," she answered. This answer certainly was wrong, and by adult logic quite "stupid." But Piaget wanted to know why this particular kind of answer had been given.

He determined that Ric knew what poppies were and what flowers were. Yet when he asked again: "Then which bunch will be bigger—the one with the flowers or the one with the poppies?" she again answered: "The one with the poppies."

Other children the same age as Ric gave similarly "illogical" answers to the same sort of questions. Piaget believes that at a certain state of development a child cannot think about the whole and the parts at the same time. When Ric thought about one she forgot about the other. Asked to compare the poppies with something, since the whole was gone, she compared them with the only thing left, the bluebells, and obviously there were more poppies.

Very young children, Piaget found, also have no notion of length. He tested them by showing them a straight ruler, and a wavy plastic "snake," the two ends of which were in line with the ends of the ruler. A child would be asked which was longer, and the usual response for a four- or five-year-old would be "the same." Then the child would be asked to trace the straight ruler and the twists and turns of the "snake" with his finger. The snake was even straightened out. But as soon as it was allowed to snap back to its wavy shape and laid out next to the ruler, the child would again assert that the two were the same length, and nothing could shake this belief. By the age of seven, however, the child is able to straighten the snake out in his mind and give the correct answer.

The concept of speed is also different for children under the age of about six than it is for adults. In a test two dolls were passed through two tunnels of different length. They entered the tunnels and arrived at the end at exactly the same moment, but if a five-year-old is asked which is faster, he will reply that their speed is the same because they got out of the tunnels at the same time. Even if he has actually watched one of the dolls moving more quickly through the tunnel than the other, the fact that they both arrived at the end at the same moment is the most important thing to him. As far as he is concerned that means that both of the dolls are moving equally fast.

Piaget himself has never claimed that his methods can be used as an alternative I.Q. test. He used his tests only in order to develop a theory of the various stages in the development of learning. But his admirers (and they are increasing among the ranks of educational psychologists) believe that his methods will ultimately provide an entirely new and more useful form of mental testing and a new mental scale.

One thing Piaget's followers have that conventional test makers do not is a theory of how intelligence develops. I.Q. tests, as we have seen, developed in a haphazard way. Piaget's tests, on the other hand, reflect an elaborate theory of mental development. In his work Piaget has carefully outlined the various stages and shown how one must follow the other. If the theory is correct, its implications for education are profound. There is no point in trying to teach a child even simple arithmetic before he or she has developed the concept of what a number is. To try would only result in frustration and probably make it harder for the child to learn arithmetic later. Teaching would have to be geared entirely to the development of the individual child, and that might mean radical changes in the whole structure of modern education.

Piaget's followers are quick to compare his tests to the more usual sort of I.Q. tests. The Piaget type of tests do not rank individuals on the basis of some sort of artificial numerical scale that is labeled intelligence. The purpose of the tests is to determine the developmental stage of the individual child. Writing in the *Saturday Review* of May 17, 1969, Gilbert Voyat, a psychologist who has occasionally collaborated with Piaget himself, says: "Piagetian tests clearly differ from typical I.Q. tests . . . I.Q. tests are essentially an additive progression of acquired skills; they allow one to place a child among children of his age and development. Piagetian tests, on the other hand . . . provide a detailed analysis of the functioning of thinking.

In short, they qualify thinking; they do not quantify it. They always respect the intelligence of a specific child."

Still it isn't hard to imagine how Piaget's theories could be used to construct a new style of I.Q. test where children were ranked in much the same way as they were in the old test. Each of the stages of development that Piaget has outlined could be given a numerical value. The scores which a child receives on various questions would be compared with a standard developed for children of that age. A ratio could be arrived at and the score reported in the same sort of numbers that are now used for I.Q. scores. According to many of Piaget's followers such a use of his theory would violate entirely the spirit of the work, which is to chart individual development not rank one child against the other. But if ranking and pigeonholing is what our society wants to do with data about thinking and intelligence, then Piaget's theories would provide an adequate vehicle. Remember that Binet once protested that his testing techniques were being misused, but that did not stop their misuse.

That, however, is a problem that we do not yet have to confront. A far more immediate problem is that, though Piaget's theories are currently very popular among educational psychologists, we are still quite a long way from knowing whether these theories are really valid. Most of Piaget's data has been reported in case history fashion, like the story of Ric and the flowers. Often Piaget provides relatively little information about the background of the subjects that he tests. Was Ric's reaction to the picture of the flowers typical of all children her age, of most, of very few? Would children of different cultural backgrounds react differently to the questions? Would a different questioner get a different set of answers? The attempt to validate Piaget's theories by mass studies with careful statistical controls have really just gotten under way.

Experimenters in places as far removed from Geneva as Central Africa and Aden in Arabia have tested children, and have gotten essentially the same results Piaget got from Swiss children. Occasionally there were variations for unusual reasons. In a village in Africa when a tester asked the question: "Do the glasses have the same amount of liquid or does one have more?" she found that the children always believed that the one that had been poured out by the experimenter contained more. The reason turned out to be that in this African society belief in witchcraft was strong, and the experimenter was regarded as a witch. If she poured the liquid the children assumed that, because of witchcraft, there must be more. But when the children were allowed to pour the liquid themselves, they answered in exactly the same way as children did in other parts of the world. These studies however are too meager and too loosely controlled to be regarded as anything more than hints.

Currently there are some intensive efforts going on both in Switzerland and in Canada to standardize a set of Piagetian tests. This work is still at its beginning stages; it would be premature to speak of Piaget's theories of development as being scientifically established.

While Jean Piaget's work on the development of intelligence is most famous, his is certainly not the only approach to the subject. A number of other psychologists who have become disenchanted with the present I.Q. tests have been attempting to devise alternate ways of probing the elusive quality called intelligence.

Much of this work concerns what is called "cognitive style," that is, how we think. David Witkin of the State University of New York has tested his subjects in a tilted room. This is an elaborate piece of equipment which consists of a small room that can be mechanically tilted to various angles either to the right or to the left. Inside the room is a chair that can also be tilted. The subject sits in the chair and the experimenter shifts the chair around and asks the subject when he thinks he is sitting up straight. It is not as easy to know when you are sitting up straight as it may sound because everything in the room looks straight, and this produces a direct and powerful conflict with the subject's inner feeling that he is sitting on a slant.

The ability to separate inner feelings from surroundings varies greatly throughout the population. The tilted room tests seems to correlate with other tests that also require the subject to separate something from its surroundings. Witkin calls those who are good at making such separations field independent and those who are not field dependent. This ability, or lack of it, appears to develop early and remain fairly constant throughout life.

What does field dependence or independence have to do with intelligence? Witkin believes that field independent people are better at understanding and solving problems which involve taking things apart. The ability appears to be partially innate and partially environmental. Girls are usually more field dependent than boys, but boys who come from an overprotective home are also heavily field dependent. Neither girls nor overprotected boys are encouraged to be independent, and this may actually affect the way in which they perceive the world, and ultimately the way in which they intellectually solve problems. In this area there is a blending of intelligence and what is often called personality.

Psychologist Riley Gardner of the Menninger Foundation tests subjects by having them sort a mass of objects into different categories. For example, a subject may be given, among other things, a saw, a hammer, a brick, and a chair. He is then asked to place the objects in any number of "logical" categories. He may put the saw, hammer, and brick in one group because they have to do with building. He might also put the saw, hammer, and chair in a group because they have to do with woodworking. Or he may put the saw and hammer in a group because both are tools, and the chair and brick in other groups. All the choices are equally logical.

Gardner found that some people tend to lump things together in large categories while others make up a large number of smaller categories. Finding similarities and differences among things is a part of learning and of intelligence.

Perhaps in the findings of these tests and others like them we will gain a greater understanding of how we think, how we learn, and ultimately of our own intelligence. On the other hand we may get quicker and better answers from studying the physiology and chemistry of the brain.

Wherever the answers lie we must end with a note of caution. The study of intelligence has been like a rat runner's maze, filled with wrong turnings and dead ends. From the worms that were supposed to learn but didn't, to I.Q. tests which were supposed to scientifically rate everyone's intelligence but don't—we have too often been confused and misled by short-lived enthusiasms. We are still just scratching the surface of a very large and important problem.

Because the word *intelligence* as it is normally used in our society is so loaded with judgments, being labeled "intelligent" or "unintelligent" is likely to have a profound effect upon an individual's life. For that reason alone, it is best for us to acknowledge how very little still we really know.

Selected
Bibliography

Alpers, A. *Dolphins: The Myth and the Mammal.* Boston: Houghton Mifflin, 1961.

Barnett, S. A. *Instinct and Intelligence: Behavior of Animals and Man.* Englewood Cliffs, N.J.: Prentice-Hall, 1967.

Butcher, H. J. *Human Intelligence: Its Nature and Assessment.* London: Methuen, 1968.

Cohen, Daniel. *Talking With the Animals.* New York: Dodd Mead, 1971.

Darwin, Charles. *The Origin of Species and The Descent of Man.* New York: Random House Modern Library Giants, 1966.

Deutsch, Martin; Katz, Irwin; & Jensen, Arthur (editors). *Social Class, Race and Psychological Development.* New York: Holt, Rinehart and Winston, 1968.

Eysenck, H. J. *Race, Intelligence and Education.* London: Temple Smith, 1971.

Fichtelius, Karl-Erik and Sjölander, Sverre. *Smarter Than Man? Intelligence in Whales, Dolphins and Humans.* New York: Pantheon, 1972.

Goodall, Jane van Lawick. *In The Shadow of Man.* Boston: Houghton Mifflin, 1971.

Gordon, Theodore. *Ideas in Conflict.* New York: St. Martins Press, 1966.

Hahn, Emily. *On the Side of the Apes.* New York: T. Y. Crowell, 1971.

Hayes, Cathy. *The Ape in Our House.* New York: Harper, 1951.

Isaacs, Nathan. *A Brief Introduction to Piaget.* New York: Agathon Press, 1972.

Jencks, Christopher and others. *Inequality: A Reassessment of The Effects of Family and Schooling in America.* New York: Scribners, 1972.

Lilly, John C. *Man and Dolphin.* New York: Doubleday, 1961.

————. *The Mind of the Dolphin.* New York: Doubleday, 1967.

McConnell, James V. (editor). *The Worm Re-Turns.* Englewood Cliffs, N.J.: Prentice-Hall, 1965.

Morris, Ramona and Desmond. *Men and Apes.* New York: McGraw-Hill, 1966.

Packard, Vance. *Animal I.Q.: The Human Side of Animals.* New York: Dial Press, 1950.

Piaget, Jean. *Child's Conception of Movement and Speed.* New York: Basic Books, 1969.

————. *Child's Conception of Number.* New York: W. W. Norton, 1965.

————. *The Origin of Intelligence in Children.* New York: W. W. Norton, 1962.

Richardson, Ken; Spears, David; & Richards, Martin (editors). *Race and Intelligence.* Baltimore, Md.: Penguin Books, 1972.

Schaller, George. *The Year of the Gorilla.* Chicago: University of Chicago Press, 1964.

Scott, John Paul. *Animal Behavior.* Chicago: University of Chicago Press, 1958.

Senna, Carl (editor). *The Fallacy of I.Q.* New York: The Third Press, 1973.

Sharp, Evelyn. *The IQ Cult.* New York: Coward, McCann, Geoghegan, 1972.

Yerkes, Robert M. and Watterson, Ada. *The Great Apes.* New Haven: Yale University Press, 1929.

Index

Picture Credits